The Dear Wild Place

The Dear Wild Place

Green spaces, community and campaigning

Emily Cutts

C|C|W|B press

First published by CCWB Press in 2019
Centre for Confidence and Well-being.
Registered Office: Abercorn House,
79 Renfrew Rd, Paisley, PA3 4DA
Registered charity number sco37080

© Emily Cutts

Cover artwork by Rhiannon Van Muysen

The moral rights of the author has been asserted.

**A catalogue record of this book is available
from the British Library**
978-0-916009-40-0

Printed and bound in UK by
Bell & Bain Ltd, Glasgow

To Quintin, Lauchlan and Jessica

POSTCARDS FROM SCOTLAND

Series editor: Carol Craig

Advisory group:
Professor Phil Hanlon, Chair,
Centre for Confidence and Well-being;
Fred Shedden

Contents

CHAPTER ONE

Introduction

THE DEAR Green Place. This is the name of a famous Glasgow novel and what Glasgow (*Glaschu*) means in Gaelic. This book is about what many in my own Glasgow community see as their Dear Wild Place – a little piece of land on the fringe of the West End, which for many years has been called the North Kelvin Meadow.

The peaceful nature of the site conceals the frenetic campaign we've had to mount in the past few years to protect this magical oasis in the heart of a busy city from housing development. I have played an important part in protecting this green space and transforming it into an outdoor community centre. The story, which follows, is my perspective on how we've managed to win what many saw as a David and Goliath struggle. For me it has often seemed like an odyssey where our battle has not just been with the Council but many of the negative features of modern life. In recounting this story I show how a grassroots initiative can address the intensive materialism of contemporary celebrity culture, improve children's lives, build a vibrant community and break down barriers caused by pronounced income inequality.

Who am I, to be explaining such an initiative? I am not an academic, nor a specialist early years worker or carer, psychologist or community worker. But I do have a blend of these things in my background. I once worked as an early years practitioner, and have a bachelors and masters degree in psychology. An important turning point for me was in 2005 when I got a job as a psychology researcher in Glasgow at the Centre for Confidence and Well-being.

The Centre was set up by Carol Craig following the interest in her ground-breaking book *The Scots' Crisis of Confidence*. She then went on to write *Creating Confidence, The Tears That Made the Clyde, The Great Takeover* and more recently *Hiding in Plain Sight: Exploring Scotland's ill health*. These books are about how culture shapes individuals' lives. The term culture includes historical forces that are often so hidden we're unaware of them as well as common assumptions and shared values.

For the first few years the Centre did a lot of work to promote Positive Psychology. I had a particular interest in this field and was one of the first students to study for an MSc in Positive Psychology in the UK at the University of East London. But Carol, the Centre more generally, and I soon became disillusioned with the limitations of this perspective seeing it as too psychological and individualistic. We became more and more convinced that a large number of factors were important for human well-being – contact with nature, connection to others, exercise, diet, equality and non-materialistic values.

I spent the next few years immersed in this well-being research compiling, almost on a daily basis, updates on the Centre's website which we called 'Emily's News'. It was only in 2011 and 2012 that I could see a way to use what I was learning to make a practical difference to people's lives. I could see how we could take a wild patch of land in our community, which was under threat from a housing development, and turn it into a community resource that could tackle some endemic contemporary problems. In fact I believe what we have achieved with our wild place is part of the Centre's legacy. Ultimately this community project had the strength to save the land from an expensive housing development. Before describing what I did, let me introduce the land in more detail.

Our Dear Wild Place

When visiting the site visitors with a keen eye will notice six rusty floodlight towers, broken fencing, and patches of red blaes on the paths and realise it was once sports pitches. Most will simply see it as a wild patch of nature transported into the city. When you enter the wooded area you feel you are in the countryside with the sounds of birds, leaves rustling and trees sheltering you. This site also harbours grassy meadow areas, raised vegetable beds, a labyrinth, an orchard and a beedookit. Usually you will find children playing and people walking their dogs.

The Meadow, as it is often called, is nearly four acres of open, and now green/wild, space in the heart of an urban setting on the edge of the Maryhill district of Glasgow. As Maryhill and nearby Kelvinside are so different in socio-economic terms it must be one of the most unequal areas in the UK. The land has never been built on and has always been a community resource. Until 1992 it was principally the playing fields for the nearby North Kelvinside School, now closed. Many older local people remember playing football on the land. Recently I met a man in his 80s who had been brought to the Meadow by his grand-daughter to see what it was like now. He played there as a child and was touched by how it had changed: it is now a natural environment with lots of trees, and many different types of people are now using the land for various activities like picnick-ing, gardening, playing and having fun. Local people had stopped playing football there 20 years ago when the then local council actively vandalised the land by driving their vans into the goal posts and destroying them. Community members still remember this shocking incident. In the early to mid-1990s Miller Homes submitted a housing plan for the land. They wanted to develop the land for residential housing, but fortunately in 1996 after a battle, the Scottish Government 'called in' the application and refused permission for development.

Since then, nature has taken over (with a bit of help in the late 90s from local residents Ian Black and others). There are now over 700 trees and a green meadow where the red blaes pitches and tennis courts were. Another local group, the Compendium Trust, are responsible for the greening of the land. While fighting to make the land into a community sports complex, they allowed nature to take over and the wildness to develop. Lucky for us now, though sad for the group at the time, their plans got knocked back at the final stages. During this time the land was used informally for dog walking and activities such as children learning to ride bikes, but it had also become a magnet for drug users and a rubbish dumping ground.

Near the end of 2008 my husband, Quintin, and I joined a litter pick-up on the land, organised by local resident Douglas Peacock. Having just moved to the area, we understood that the site was under threat: once more Glasgow City Council wanted to sell the land for expensive housing and had chosen a preferred developer. We collected dozens of bin bags of rubbish, a box of needles and medical equipment, some furniture and other larger items. Douglas and other locals had formed the North Kelvin Meadow Campaign and they continued to meet for the next couple of years to pick litter and garden. They put in raised beds for people to grow fruit and vegetables. Douglas still manages the raised beds and volunteers. During these years Quintin and I helped out with the odd litter pick. In this period, we mainly were observers as we had very young children, and we also had a spell away working and living in the USA. The campaign group gathered several hundred supporters via a petition, and email list, and investigated the policies and procedures of the Council and the history of the preferred developer. In particular, group members started to develop an argument against building that made use of the Council's own planning regulations on open space and the disposal of sports pitches.

Prior to the latest planning application being submitted I had been thinking of initiating activities on the land, but without the impetus of the threat to the site's future this might have come to nothing. The main catalyst for my involvement came in May 2012 when New City Vision Ltd, the Council's preferred developer, submitted a planning application for a high-end housing development on the whole site. As Glasgow City Council owned the land, if they approved this application, they stood to make about £10,000,000. New houses would also generate significant funds for the Council in council tax.

When the planning application was submitted my energy and motivation for doing something with the site increased tenfold. Something shifted inside me. I had a strong vision for how we could implement some of the research findings I had learned about at the Centre and how we could create a new way of doing things. What surprised me was my faith and optimism that we could save the land. I had never believed in anything more. I just 'knew' that, despite the odds, we could save the site from development. This belief is what carried me through some hard times and kept me going when I was tempted to give up or do something else.

At this point I had no idea how this initiative would take over my life – not just for weeks but months and years. At this stage we only had 28 days to beat the planning deadline. But this didn't faze me – I thought this was long enough to change minds and involve people. Of course, minds have changed and people have become involved but it has taken almost seven years of continual effort. But while my timing was a little out, the premise wasn't.

So what was my idea? The key issue in my mind was that an academic argument based on planning policies, would not be enough to stop this multi-million pound juggernaut. I was convinced that only an empowered community, in love with the land, could have a real effect. And to do this, citizens from near and far had to get on the land, use it regularly, and begin to develop that deep affection for it. In parallel I could see that this bit of wild, largely untended land had the potential not just to stimulate community engagement but also address local needs. I wanted much more than a nimbyist 'don't build here' campaign or gardening groups – I believed that we could win this battle by creating something lasting for our community. This would be done through drawing on the knowledge I gained during my time at the Centre and applying two core concepts: *care* and *connection*. As you will see shortly, care and connection have been at the heart of our grassroots community project.

Folk have joked with me about how we've spent these years planning and leading a battle, or waging a war, but in fact this analogy works rather well. By encouraging local people to care about the land, my energy has been magnified many hundreds of times and we have ended up winning the battle against housing on the land. That could only have happened by hundreds of people working together, making connections, friendships and forming a community based around shared values. All of this was acted out on the shared stage of the land.

Battle plan – making people care

I wanted people to care as much as I did about the land. If people cared they would be more motivated to take action to save the land. Over the years there had been various campaigns but I felt much of this activity had been rather abstract. To make local people really care they would need to connect with the land in some way and feel the benefit of the space for them, or for their family and friends. Only once they realised its true value would they really care about such a space.

So how did we get people to use the land and to care deeply about it? Well it was something of an uphill struggle. After a couple of years of organised litter pick-ups, the North Kelvin Meadow Campaign had done a great job and the land was safe. However, many locals still did not perceive it as such, using it only as a cut-through or for dog walking. In fact at that stage many had never been on the land at all. When you are on the land you can appreciate its beauty, but from the outside the land looked somewhat derelict. The wooded tennis court area was almost never used and even people who did use the Meadow to walk through were unaware of the Wood as they stayed only on the open paths. Schools didn't use the land because there were safety issues and there was still a lot of dog mess. Many locals thought the land was unsafe for children.

Many members of the community were also very pessimistic about the chances of stopping the housing development. Not only did the Council stand to make millions from the sale of the land but our area already had a great deal of green space such as the immaculate Botanic Gardens or the walkway along the Kelvin. This is why many people thought that the chances of saving this place were slim. However, I always knew that this wild place was different and much more valuable to the community.

I believed the key was to get people from near and far on the land. I organised a series of events for children and the community, every two weeks, and then monthly. I organised mass den building, recycling events, bow and arrow making and much more. All free. Walking from nursery to nursery I invited parents, carers, teachers to use the land. We also became highly skilled at trowelling dog mess as this was one of the main barriers to people coming to the land. Events got more eye-catching: lighting up the Meadow for Halloween; bringing in reindeer at Christmas. These activities had a dual purpose – to entice more folk on the land as well as raise the profile in the media. The *Evening Times* became our friend and the *Herald, Sun, Scotsman, Guardian, Times, Daily Record* and *Private Eye* also gave us lots of useful coverage. As we could see the importance of getting young people outside on this piece of land we started to call a portion of the site 'the Children's Wood' but there were also events aimed at getting people involved in the wider Meadow. However, the Children's Wood title has often been attached to activities which are not about children.

Many more local people came on board. People baked cakes to sell to raise money, locals volunteered to help out at events, people litter picked before events and handed out flyers. Many locals visited councillors to put over our arguments. One way or another hundreds of people took up the opportunities we created, volunteered and became part of the larger campaign.

Because I could see clearly how this space had the potential to address many current social problems, I thought that convincing others would be easy. It wasn't. Neither was it easy to encourage people to be optimistic about our chances of success. Clearly there is an entrenched view that Goliath usually beats David in real life. Hence, so much of the work over the last seven years has been about communicating the argument to various groups including the wider community, education establishments and the Council. To help us make these arguments we involved various experts in some of our events to help make the argument for us – e.g. Sue Palmer, who set up Upstart Scotland and is now an expert on play, and Carol Craig who is an expert on well-being. We also involved local teachers and academics. Some well-known celebrities also supported us. For example, the Scottish actress Kate Dickie came to the site and supported us in the press. Writers Alasdair Gray and Liz Lochhead came to an event and read stories. Actor Tam Dean Burn read *The Gruffalo* and food writer Josceline Dimbleby attended an event to judge a 'bake outdoors' competition and signed our petition.

An army of volunteers, three on-line petitions, hundreds of events, a three month vigil in George Square, local and national awards, countless newspaper articles both local and national, and television appearances meant that we managed to run an extremely high profile campaign. In January 2013 we submitted a petition to the Scottish Government, including 3435 signatures, asking them to call in the planning application. A few months later the Scottish Government notified Glasgow City Council that they reserved the right to call in the planning application should the Council be minded to approve it.

The battle intensifies

Glasgow City Council, with so much money at stake, were not deterred. In 2015 in their draft for City Plan 3, the new city-wide planning document against which all planning applications would now be judged, the Council proposed to rezone North Kelvin Meadow as building land. If successful, this would be a green light for the New City Vision plan for expensive housing on the site. But we had so many people mobilised to save the land that we were able to fight back. 179 objection letters were lodged and we mounted a further online petition which gathered 1875 responses. Under planning rules this number of objections meant that the Council had to refer its proposal to the Scottish Government.

Meanwhile, on January 26th 2016 Glasgow City Council's Planning Committee visited the North Kelvin Meadow and Children's Wood. This was ahead of the Council Planning Committee meeting that would determine whether they would give planning permission to New City Vision for housing development. Hundreds of people came out in the pouring rain to support the campaign. This included local nursery schools, local businesses, head teachers, campaigners such as Sue Palmer and Darren McGarvey as well as the actor Tam Dean Burn, who was now patron of the campaign. After the site visit we headed in hired buses to the City Chambers. Most of our supporters stayed outside and the rest of us crammed into the committee room inside the City Chambers. The situation was intense – years of work were now coming to a head. During the committee meeting I spoke and so did several other community members such as Ralph Green who was one of our trustees. We could hear all our supporters outside the Chambers in George Square singing and chanting support for the campaign. As we expected though, later that day the developers were granted outline planning permission for the land. However, on the same day the Children's Wood was also granted planning permission for a community park and garden. This was all thanks to architect Alex Macgregor. Alex had drawn up an alternative planning application for us and submitted this on our behalf. This showed the City Council that we meant business and had a strategy for the long-term use of the site. I believe this move by Alex was pivotal in our campaign, and was strengthened by our previous petition which prompted the Government to send a letter to the Council advising of a possible call-in. The success of that petition, and the others, couldn't have happened without the thousands of people passionate about the land.

Our success meant that we now had the confidence to pursue our alternative plan. However, the developers had an agreement with the Council that if they gained full planning permission they would buy the land and build on it. Only the Scottish Government could now prevent this, by acting on their earlier letter to the Council advising that they would consider calling-in the developers planning propopsal. We had to ensure this would happen. Our campaign gathered momentum and we decided to focus on getting a public inquiry or hearing. Local resident Kristin Mojsiewicz helped mount a postcard campaign asking for the application to be called in by the Scottish Government. The Government have the power to call in and investigate applications when they are concerned that a local authority may not be observing its own policy and planning procedures correctly. The subsequent investigation can be through a Public Hearing or a Public Inquiry. We were asking the Government for a Public Inquiry since we believed it to be more thorough, but we would be happy if we got either. Over 6,000 people signed our petition asking for a call in and people sent postcards from near and far to us for delivery to the Scottish Government. We received postcards from Alasdair Gray, poet Benjamin Zephaniah, Josceline Dimbleby and from people as far away as Squaws Peak in Arizona and Melbourne Australia. *The Herald* also published an open letter from us asking for a Public Inquiry. On Tuesday 1st March 2016 some of us went to the Scottish Government to deliver the postcards. We were joined by local residents and nursery school children from schools in Maryhill. Also with us on the day was retired plumber Jim Divers who handed over the folder. He had been emptying the bins on the land every day since the North Kelvin Meadow Campaign started, and still does.

The Scottish Government responded favourably and scheduled a Public Hearing. Though this wasn't the Public Inquiry we were asking for, nonetheless we were delighted. This was scheduled for 6th September 2016. Before this, however, on 22nd June, the news came through from the Scottish Government that the Council's proposal to change the status of the land in the draft City Plan 3 had been deleted by the appointed reporter thanks to our previous campaigning. He recommended that the land should be designated as open space, with all the protections that brings, writing:

> The land at Clouston Street is a highly valued open space which is well used and maintained by the local community, and which should continue to be safeguarded for that purpose. Its development for housing would be in conflict with planning policies which seek to protect such areas. I have therefore decided to modify the Proposed Plan by deleting Housing Proposal H023.

This was obviously a huge boost to our campaign.

The Public Hearing was held in the Maryhill Burgh Halls, with a different reporter in charge. We had sent in a summary of our objections to housing, based on both the Council's own planning regulations and also on the overwhelming community evidence and feedback. The Council were required to demonstrate how they could both build on the land *and* adhere to their own policies while doing so, which, for example, required provision of like-for-like land in the area. We were seated in a U-shape of tables facing both the Council and the developers, and the reporter sat at a table between us. As we had so much at stake it was a very intense experience for all of us. Many of us spoke and we were joined by our supporters such as Alex Macgregor, local head teachers, Marguerite Hunter Blair from Play Scotland, a local Wyndford mum of three autistic children, and Dr Katherine Jones from the RSPB. Scotland's Children's Commissioner Tam Baillie sent in a letter of support.

The hearing lasted two days and there were some highs and lows. The weight of support behind us from respected people and organisations, who recognised the benefit of the land, as well as a strong planning-based argument, were enormously important to our cause and gave us great hope. But, given the combined clout of the Council and the developer, there were also times when our hope of stopping the development wavered. On the second day the reporter requested a site visit. Given the work we had been doing for years in building our campaign it was pretty easy for us to get many people onto the land quickly. When we showed the reporter around he was welcomed by hundreds of people who loved the land. He could see children playing, people chatting to one another, families picnicking and so on. For me there was one incredibly memorable moment. A man stopped and asked to speak to the reporter. He said, 'I'm a teacher and I cannot tell you enough how this land supports the learning and development of children. There is nothing like this and it's a model and example for other areas. Please reject these plans.' This spontaneous interaction summed up what the land meant to the education of our children and young people and how important the site was for inspiring others to make change.

War strategy – creating and sustaining connection

Once we heard that we had won, on December 21st 2016, and that the land would remain undeveloped, we felt elated. The reporter argued that this was because building would mean a loss of open space with inappropriate mitigation for all the multifunctional uses, as well as a loss of biodiversity.

This was an important win for people power. Thousands of local people had been involved in so many different ways – from leading events to simply turning up on a rainy day and splashing in puddles. Their involvement truly demonstrated that people cared and loved the land, and that our battle strategy had indeed succeeded. We weren't the only ones overjoyed. 'I've just heard the wonderful news that the Children's Wood has been saved. Bravo to our community for all their tireless campaigning. It's the best Christmas present ever,' said *Game of Thrones* actor, Kate Dickie.

However, some people worried that now the campaign to save the land was over we would lose our shared vision and sense of purpose. But this wasn't my concern. I knew that there was a much bigger war to be fought involving lots of different battles: the battle to improve mental health and reduce loneliness, for example, or the on-going battle against the various factors in our culture which undermine children's well-being. In short, this on-going war wasn't about fighting the Council about the use of the land. Now we had won that battle, we could concentrate on a bigger war about wider societal problems such as materialist values and the restrictions on children's freedom to play outside.

The remainder of this book is about these other battles we have faced or are facing and how we're using our wild place to win each of those battles.

I believe that community wild spaces can play a vital role in making the type of change we need to bring about healthier lives. Place is very important to people and can make the difference between living your life and having a life *worth* living. Wild space can help people to know themselves. It can also bring people out of dark holes and give meaning and purpose in a sometimes scary world.

In recent years we have heard a lot about the importance of green space and of course this is vital for communities and individuals. But we hear much less about the importance of wild spaces or what I often refer to as 'social wild space' or 'multifunctional community open wild space'. Whatever its name what is needed is a local natural semi-wild space within walking distance of a community that serves to meet different needs within that community.

Nature and the community are as important as each other. Indeed I passionately believe that such community wild spaces provide the opportunity to challenge some of the more toxic elements of our culture. There is so much research showing that our contact with nature is declining and our connection with the digital world increasing. This is having a hugely detrimental effect on our, and particularly our children's, well-being. As I shall show in later chapters of this book, community access to wild space is one of the things we need to improve mental health, reduce loneliness, and break down generational barriers. Nature is important, and more needed now than we could ever have imagined. This has nothing to do with saving distant rainforests (though that is vital too), and much more to do with saving each one of us, right here on our doorstep.

My community has changed and is much more receptive to the outdoors and now knows the value of wild spaces. But we are not typical. I dream of seeing what we have achieved here in Maryhill happening in areas right across Glasgow and Scotland, each initiated by the local community and started by someone with a vision and courage to do something different.

I hope our success with the Children's Wood and North Kelvin Meadow will set a precedent for other communities, that it will inspire them to do something similar. I hope it will be easier the second, third, fourth and fiftieth time around for other communities to find and protect their 'dear wild place'.   □

CHAPTER TWO

Wild space – the unsung hero

> This site may not have eagles and adders, natterjacks
> or nightjars, curlews or corncrakes: but it has worms
> and robins and beetles and sparrows and it is where
> people living in city flats can get out and get close to
> nature. Even in the Dear Green Place, North Kelvin
> Meadow and the Children's Wood stand out as
> special, because of what the local community have
> made of it. We need more places in our cities where
> people can get close to nature not fewer.
>
> Dr Katherine Jones, RSPB

WHEN the planning application went in for housing on our Dear Wild Place I wanted to highlight how the 'unsung hero' of wild space could tackle issues which are both global and local. I wanted to show the Council and the Scottish Government an alternative to building that would preserve our cherished land and ultimately deliver better value to Glasgow citizens than a land sale and council tax receipts.

This chapter summarises some of the health issues we face and explores the research evidence on how access to green space can help address these problems. I give various ideas on how to put the research into practice and outline how we applied this learning in our own community.

Major public health Issues

There's a growing public health crisis in many Western countries and Scotland is no exception. Of course, I'm referring to rising levels of mental and physical health problems. Globally more than 300 million people suffer from depression and it's currently the leading cause of disability worldwide. This is set to increase. Over the last decade depression levels have increased by 20 per cent, and it's a major contributor to the overall global burden of disease. In Scotland, one in three appointments with a GP relates to a mental health problem. One in four people in Scotland will experience a significant mental health problem at some point in their lives.

People in the most deprived areas are more than three times as likely to spend time in hospital because of a mental health issue, compared to someone living in a less deprived area. We also know that those living in areas of deprivation and who experience additional life challenges, such as unemployment, financial hardship, family break-up and social isolation, are particularly vulnerable to mental health problems. Antidepressant prescribing has skyrocketed over the last ten years. During 2017/2018 alone, 900,000 people in Scotland were prescribed at least one antidepressant. Over the last decade, antidepressant prescribing in Scotland has risen by almost three million items a year! Anxiety disorders, such as panic attacks, are also increasing steadily. The financial cost of mental health in the UK is in excess of £10 billion per year and the system is struggling to cope with the rising demand.

Inactivity and obesity are also major public health issues. In Scotland it is estimated that low physical activity contributes to around 2,500 deaths per year and costs the NHS £94 million annually. Low levels of physical activity can lead to cardiovascular disease, cancer, obesity and being overweight, diabetes, mental illness and poor musculoskeletal health.

Children's physical inactivity and obesity are pressing problems in Scotland. Diet is undoubtedly part of the problem but lack of exercise is a major contributor. So is the fact that Scotland has an indoor culture. For example, television viewing in Scotland is higher than in any other country in the UK. The average Scot watches television for 3 hours 46 minutes per day.

It was only really when I started bringing schools and the community to the Children's Wood and North Kelvin Meadow that I realised how bad the problem was. I suddenly met children who never played outside and who reported high levels of TV and computer game use. I met those who were overweight and unhappy. I met adults who never spent time outside and who were I felt suffering the consequences.

Misunderstanding the value of spending time in green space

Imagine there was a secret weapon – a tool that could prevent mental illness, improve health, build resilience, boost learning and education and make people happy. Then imagine that this weapon has no downside or cost. It's hard to imagine something so powerful. This secret weapon does exist and it's in the heart of our communities. It's not a pill or a potion. It's not therapy or classes. The weapon we have readily at our disposal to counteract mental ill health is our unloved, underused outdoor community spaces: our parks and gardens, and our small patches of wild spaces. These are on our doorstep and waiting to be claimed and used.

This is not a well-understood or much employed argument. People tend to think of nature as providing the context for nice activities or hobbies. Many think it is a luxury for those who can make the time to get outdoors. However, nature is good for *all* of us. We have this wonderful and powerful resource around us, yet we do not embrace it as a tool for making positive change. This realisation was one of the main motivations for me in the campaign to save the land from development. I could see the potential of our Dear Wild Place to improve mental health and well-being. Both the Scottish Government and Glasgow Council had developed various policies and strategies for getting people outside. For example, the Scottish Government's document 'Good Places Better Health' states that in order for people (children specifically in this case) to develop a strong association with the natural world it is important that green spaces are close to the home, within a range of 300 metres and that young children spend more time in them.

But while many official documents highlight the benefits of nature for people's mental and physical health, and talk about the importance of access, I could not see where this was happening. No one I knew had ready access to these types of experiences. My thinking was that if these policies were not being applied in our community then I would just start applying them and help to implement some of the existing policies and strategies.

I could see that our Dear Wild Place had the potential to bring people to the land and support the prevention and alleviation of mental health issues. I also wanted to show the Council that there is strong evidence to support this claim. But before summarising some of this evidence I want to say something about my own academic subject – psychology.

The rise of ecopsychology

In 2006 I attended the Gallup Positive Psychology Summit in Washington DC and went to a lecture by Tal Ben Shahar, a Professor at Harvard University who teaches a course on happiness. At that time his course was the largest subscribed subject in the history of the university, beating introduction to economics. To this day the course is still oversubscribed. I'll never forget this lecture since it introduced so many concepts I am interested in, in such a simple way, but with a slow and mindful delivery – a signature feature of his approach.

During his lecture Tal laid out the evidence in support of the positive link between exercise and mental health. Exercise, according to research, can be as effective for mild to moderate depression as antidepressants. But Tal went on to make two even more important points. Exercise is so important to how we feel that *not* being physically active is depressing. What's more, exercise is not just an antidepressant, it can also make people feel good and improve well-being. In other words, taking exercise can both reduce negative feelings *and* more importantly build positive emotions. Even better is the fact that exercise has no real side effects the way that drugs do.

While I was very impressed by Tal's talk I realised when I became involved in the campaign for the Children's Wood that he had failed to mention anything about the importance of nature and being in the green world. According to what he said exercise in a gym or on concrete pavements was as good for you as being out in nature. Intuitively I knew this wasn't right.

Now I know that mainstream psychology has been blind to the importance of nature. Theodore Roszak is one of the founders of the growing movement called ecopsychology. He explains that traditionally psychology has looked at individuals as subjects divorced from their environment and from the natural world. It employs a methodology which fails to address the natural ecology of the universe – the fact that everything is connected.

Psychology has thus denied the importance of the world to mental health, focusing instead on the individual's subjective state. If the individual is mentally unhealthy then this is seen as the result of the individual's thoughts and emotions, which must be 'cured' through various therapeutic means. But as the American psychologist James Hillman points out:

> The 'bad' place I am 'in' may refer not only to a depressed mood or an anxious state of mind; it may refer to a sealed-up office tower where I work, a set-apart suburban subdivision where I sleep, or the jammed freeway on which I commute between the two.

Ecopsychologists are particularly interested in how the green environment, and the sense of connection to nature, is important for human well-being. And, as we shall see, they are right to stress the importance of the green world for good mental, and physical, health.

The positive influence of nature on health and well-being

There is now a large amount of evidence on the positive influence of nature on health and well-being. Here is a brief overview:

Mental health
Studies show that living in a green neighbourhood is strongly associated with good mental health and green space can help

counteract psychological distress. Researchers have looked at the effects of increasing exposure to green space and how such exposure can improve mental health. All socioeconomic groups reaped these benefits as did both genders. People living in urban areas with more green space have been shown to have a reduced level of stress and improved well-being compared to those with poorer availability of green space. Moving to an area with higher levels of greenery has also been associated with improvements in mental health.

Given these results it is hardly surprising that people who live in communities with more green space have lower levels of depression, anxiety and stress. Other research has found that the quality of, and access to, green space is associated with reduced psychological distress. In a study in four European cities the researchers found that spending more time in green space is associated with improved mental health and vitality independent of cultural and climatic context. A 2006 study found that contact with nature could prevent mental health disorders, if this contact happened alongside physical activity and good social connections.

Depression
Another research study showed that people living close to trees and green spaces are less likely to be dependent on anti-depressants. A study by Stanford University researchers found that people who walked in a natural area for 90 minutes, as opposed to participants who walked in an urban setting, showed decreased activity in the subgenual prefrontal cortex, a brain region active during rumination (repetitive thought focused on negative emotions). This brain area is associated with depression. A study in 2013 by researchers from the University of Essex published by MIND found that walking in nature reduced

depression scores and increased a sense of well-being. People who regularly use parks near to their home reported fewer symptoms of depression.

I have often thought about Tal Ben Shahar's reframing of the evidence on physical activity and mental health and I can see how we can apply this frame to mental health and access to the natural world. Thus we can see that *not* accessing nature is making people depressed, anxious and unhappy. Spending time in nature is nature's own medicine for mild to moderate depression. It doesn't cost a thing. Antidepressants, a common treatment for depression, are the only option in some cases and have their place but they can have many side effects. Green therapy by contrast does not leave people with terrible side effects apart from possibly mud, dirt and the occasional cut and bruise. The added effect of nature is that it can also boost positive emotions, well-being and resilience. So just as with exercise not accessing nature is depressing but being in green space can make us feel good *and* reduce negative emotions.

Cognitive benefits

A 2015 study published in the *British Journal of Sports Medicine* found that walking a half-mile through a park reduces brain fatigue. Scientists have known for some time that the human brain's ability to stay focused is limited. This means that the constant noise and demands of living in a city can easily lead to mental fatigue. EEG studies have found that a short walk in a green space impacts on brain activity; some areas of the brain which are associated with enhanced relaxation and restoration are active. The study found that a walk in the park is different from walking in a concrete area; people who walked in the park showed increased thinking skills.

Attention Deficit Hyperactivity Disorder (ADHD)

Research shows that children who have access to green environments display improved behavioural development and reduced ADHD problems. Greenness surrounding home and school was associated with improved thinking skills (better progress in working memory and reduced inattentiveness) in schoolchildren. The association was partly mediated by reduced exposure to air pollution. A number of other studies have demonstrated the positive impact of green space exposure on ADHD.

Health

One of the now most famous set of studies into nature and health showed that when patients had a view of nature from their hospital window they recovered quicker. They also needed less medication and their physical health improved more than those who didn't have a green view. A natural view also has a positive impact on blood pressure levels. Natural spaces in general are associated with reduced blood pressure, less self reported stress, lower levels of the stress hormone cortisol and increases in positive mood. For example, when people spend time in woodland environments they have fewer stress hormones and lower blood pressure than those in a city environment. Exposure to green space reduces chronic stress in adults living in deprived urban neighbourhoods. Cortisol measures have also demonstrated the stress reducing effects of gardening, suggesting that such activities in green space may be particularly restorative.

The impact of nature on our health starts before we're even born. It has been shown that exposure to green spaces during pregnancy has beneficial effects on *in utero* development. Various studies have found a link between access to green space during pregnancy and increased birth weight and this health advantage lasts the entire life course.

Healthy behaviours

Even just showing people pictures of nature can increase positive emotions. Looking at nature promotes health-oriented behaviours in people such as less desire to engage in unhealthy activities like smoking. But actually being in nature is better.

Other studies show that contact with nature can reduce the propensity for aggression – aggression and violence levels are lower in areas with local green space. Areas with more trees and greenery have lower rates of violence and crime. In 2001 Kuo and Sullivan studied the inhabitants of an urban public housing complex in Chicago, and tested the hypothesis that nearby nature reduces the propensity for aggression. They interviewed long-term female residents of the apartment complex and found that levels of aggression and violence were significantly lower among individuals who had some nearby nature outside their apartments than among their counterparts who lived in barren conditions, and that residents living in greener settings demonstrated reliably better performance on measures of 'attentional functioning'.

Theories explaining these benefits

There are two main theories underlying the health benefits of exposure to nature. The first is 'psycho-physiological stress reduction theory' which simply proposes that contact with nature, such as a walk in green space or viewing a natural scene, is healing. According to this theory our capacity to recover from stressful events is enhanced by exposure to nature. Being in nature can reduce high levels of stress by inducing a more relaxed mental state. This impacts on the nervous system by reducing stress levels and increasing feelings of relaxation and well-being.

The second theory, 'attention restorative theory', on the other hand asserts that nature impacts on our attention span. We possess two levels of attention: direct attention and indirect attention. Direct attention is used for effortful thought like maths or report writing and is a limited resource. When focusing on a task we can only use this type of attention for so long as it depletes. Indirect attention is effortless and involuntary and can restore our focused attention when it gets fatigued. This happens through the natural environment, and so it can improve performance in cognitively challenging tasks.

Ecopsychologists take a different approach. They argue that human beings are hardwired to need nature. In this respect they draw on the biologist E.O. Wilson's idea of 'biophilia'. Ecopsychologists believe that over the centuries we have become more distant from nature and that this is injuring human health and well-being as well as the planet. Helping people to connect with nature can therefore help with the rising tide of mental ill health as well as give us the impetus to lead more environmentally sustainable lives.

Case studies: putting research into action

Nature has many different and positive results for people's health and well-being and its importance is now being recognised in the medical world but we are still a long way from mainstream social prescribing. However, there are some encouraging programmes and initiatives to foster health and well-being through physical activity and contact with nature. For example, in Shetland GPs are now prescribing hill walking, walks along the beach or bird watching for people suffering from long term mental and physical health problems. The NHS Forest Project in Oxford is aiming to increase patients' use of local green space and woodland. In our area we have one or two doctors who prescribe time on North Kelvin Meadow and the Wood for mental and physical health issues and we are working to get more medical professionals to see the value of this approach.

In 2008 the New Economics Foundation (NEF) published a document that summarised the research on well-being. They came up with five main pathways to build what they call 'mental capital'. They argue that well-being is about personal experiences in one's life such as feelings of contentment, joy, curiosity and enjoyment. The way the person functions in the world is also important and this includes relationships with others, having control over your life and adopting a sense of meaning and purpose. NEF also set out five evidence based actions for people to undertake to improve well-being.

> **Learn** – try something new, take up an old interest, set a challenge, do something that takes you out of your comfort zone.
>
> **Connect** – build social relationships and networks, connect with family. Speak to neighbours, colleagues and friends.
>
> **Give** – plant some seeds, volunteer, be kind to a stranger, be thankful.

Take notice – remark on the unusual, be observant, join a mindfulness session, photograph something that takes your eye, savour the moment.

Be active – go for a walk, garden, cycle, play games, dance.

The Conservation Volunteers (TCV) created an outdoor programme around these five ways to well-being called 'Wild Ways Well'. At North Kelvin Meadow we piloted a programme on the land which built on previous pilots developed between TCV and the mental health charity Mind and trialled by TCV in Cumbernauld in 2016. Pilots involved local partners and beneficiaries including the Scottish Association for Mental Health, Neighbourhood Networks and local high schools. Pilot projects explored a range of formats to find the most effective, practical and enjoyable. The pilot report (Jan 2017) concluded:

> By bringing people together to enjoy and develop an awareness of local nature and wildlife. . . Wild Ways Well creates and maintains positive social relationships; building physical and psychological strength and resilience with benefits for individuals and the whole community. . . Wild Ways Well promotes purpose and participation enabling people to build self-esteem and confidence levels.

We piloted a programme with the TCV early in 2018 which proved to be successful. This has led us to further develop this idea and provide a long term mental health approach, integrating ideas from the Five Ways to Well-being and other approaches.

Here are some examples of things those of us involved with the Children's Wood have done over the years that fit into the Five Ways to Well-being model:

Learn: Train teachers in how to use the outdoors, train community members in Forest School approaches and other skills. Provide opportunities to learn from each other e.g. skills share events, gardening sessions, community training events, film shows, running workshops, inviting 'experts' to speak to the community.

Connect: Organise regular events such as gardening, schools sessions and playgroups. Have an open space available 24 hours a day to provide regular opportunities to connect with people. Invite people to use 'their' land. Encourage a sense of ownership through the way we talk about the space – 'your land' 'our land' 'our back garden' etc.

Give: Opportunities to volunteer, plant something, fix things on the land.

Take notice: Use Facebook as a tool to show things or highlight aspects of the land. Use different areas of the land to show a different side to the space. Show people the simple things and encourage appreciation of them, whether that is an interesting flower or the way the trees move in the wind. Encourage photography and art.

Be active: Provide the opportunity for outdoor games, gardening, conservation work, building things, walking to the land, walking around the land, climbing trees.

There are now a range of therapies and treatments for people thanks to the rise of ecopsychology and what people now call 'green therapy'. This approach shifts the emphasis away from an individualistic focus to the interconnectedness between the person and the natural world. And this is what we are promoting.

Research Hub

Academic researchers find it very difficult to find real world participants for their research projects and this is why they often use undergraduates. So when Professor Niamh Stack from the Psychology Department at the University of Glasgow got in touch to invite us to collaborate on research involving people using the land we immediately agreed. Her students have now worked with local schools, mental health groups, local people and volunteers. This research hub has been mutually beneficial: the students are involved in a meaningful piece of work but we also benefit from research studies which show the positive effects people can experience as a result of using the land. Some of the unpublished, but significant, research findings show that attention span, self-esteem or creativity improved after people spent time in the Meadow or Wood.*

Theory into practice

If all we do is go for a walk or spend time in our local green space then we are still gaining the benefits of being in nature. This can be powerful. We don't need to do anything special outdoors for that positive benefit to occur.

However, having regular groups and activities for people to go to can further enhance the benefit of nature for people's mental health and well-being as well as boosting physical activity. This is because regular activities encourage people outside more and increase the opportunities to get outside, reduce loneliness

---

*To access a summary of this research go to *The Dear Wild Place* section of www.postcardsfromscotland.co.uk

and brings generations together. Regular activity can also help to build friendships, develop new skills and encourage people to take an active role in their local wild spaces.

The research discussed so far supports the value of communities having a local green space, like ours, available to them. These studies support the importance of nature for mental health and well-being. The good news is that there is the motivation for social prescribing among those who can do this, and local green spaces and communities can help to overcome these barriers through running sessions and walking people to the land. There is a great resource in our area – as well as across Glasgow – called Community Links. The Community Links workers are based in health care centres and support patients to access resources. This can mean that Link workers can do things like meet patients and walk them to activities. This is particularly helpful for those more vulnerable patients, or those who are low in confidence. For example, someone high in social anxiety might need that extra support to get to a group meeting.

We have also witnessed people using the land in ways we wouldn't have anticipated. For example, one highly stressed woman I know arranged to meet her social worker on the land. Walking side by side, rather than in a face-to-face meeting, coupled with being in green space rather than a stuffy office, had a calming effect on her and meant that she was much more relaxed and cooperative. Another friend and local resident adopted a child and used the space to help build trust and connection with the two-year-old. She says that being in the space, playing, 'provided a natural way for us to bond'.

The wider problem

The problem is that while there are a number of great techniques and activities to connect people with nature and to nurture mental health, there are very few of them currently being used in Scotland. Or, if there are such activities, they are not community based and/or all year round. In short, ecotherapy is not widely practised in Scotland. If there are mental health courses they are often located across the city and possibly only on for short periods of time. Sometimes the programmes change locations and end up being further away for people. This can then make participation too challenging for those who are suffering from mental health issues. Often even just the simplest of tasks can be daunting for someone in the throes of mental illness or trying to recover. Having mental health resources within walking distance of communities can help to prevent mental health problems or people from relapsing. It can also change people's day-to-day lives by introducing them to their local wild/green spaces.

There are other, often more intractable problems, for all of us: there is a constant pull and conflict between the culture we live in and our ability to get outdoors. It's not enough just to have parks and green spaces. We know this because Glasgow has many parks and gardens yet we still have very low rates of physical activity and outdoor time. It is the way we live our lives (the prevailing culture) which is undermining our ability to get outside.

Here are some of the main barriers to spending more time outdoors: lack of time; fear; stranger danger; car use; screen time; TV viewing; the lure of indoor activities such as shopping, hobbies and club membership; comfortable homes.

Making it easier for people to access their local spaces will improve the amount of time people spend outdoors. Community projects have the added benefit of not being bound up with red tape and therefore it can be easier for them to deliver such programmes. Communities like ours can just get on and do it. What's more, communities can recognise more easily what's required in their area and how best to attract people. ☐

CHAPTER THREE

Childhood

My poor kids, they spend so much time in cars these days, or inside shopping centres. . . even at the parks they're being 'sold to' all the time, whether it's a burger or ice cream van in the Botanics, or a bouncy castle in Kelvingrove. We're lucky to have such amenities, yes, but luckier still just to have somewhere quiet and unspoilt, where they can just kick about and be under no pressure to consume anything more than the brambles. I really don't think you can understand how much that means to children in our pressure cooker cities.

Local parent,
The Children's Wood and North Kelvin Meadow

CHILDHOOD is not the idyllic and carefree time we're told it is. Growing up in Scotland has become an indoor, sedentary and often toxic experience for many children. Our children are suffering; plagued by mental and physical health problems. When I had my own children I became acutely aware of the lack of children playing outside in our community and the disconnection between children and nature. I had read about the restrictions being placed on children's opportunities to play outside, and that children were no longer playing outdoors, but the reality was shocking. When we started to bring people and children to the Meadow and Wood for outdoor play and fun they confirmed this problem. The level of materialism also struck me. Childhood is now filled with advertising and parents are constantly encouraged to buy and pay for child-related activities and objects.

I could see the potential of the North Kelvin Meadow and Wood for bringing children outside into nature and connecting them to both the space and their community. This could help to counteract the prevalent indoor lifestyle and materialism. This chapter is about the problems of childhood, why children need outdoor community play spaces and how to get children outside for play and learning.

The rise of sedentary childhood

Children are much more housebound than they were even just a few decades ago. In 2012 the National Trust published a report by Stephen Moss showing how children's behaviour towards outdoor play and life within their community has changed. Children's roaming radiuses – how far children will travel unsupervised from home – have decreased by almost 90 per cent since the 1970s. The report also found that children are outdoors less often than they used to be. In 1971, 80 per cent of 7 and 8-year-old children walked to school without an adult and this reduced to 10 per cent in 20 years. Only one in three 10-year-olds has ever been to a shop or park by themselves.

Further findings from the report revealed that only a third of children could identify a magpie – the same number that could identify a Dalek. And less than one in ten children regularly played in wild spaces. In 2012 nature broadcaster Chris Packham observed: 'The children out in the woods, out in the field, enjoying nature on their own – they're extinct.'

It is not just children's contact with nature that's suffering but also their physical activity. There is now a global alliance of 49 countries collecting data on children's activity and they publish their findings annually under the banner of 'Active Healthy Kids Report'. The most recent report for Scotland in 2018 is worrying. The standardised Grading Framework, applied across the 49 countries, ranges from A to F and is calculated on the percentage of children meeting a benchmark. Scotland scored reasonably well – B – when it comes to children being involved in organised sport but scored badly – a D minus – on sedentary behaviour. This involves too much screen time, particularly in deprived areas. Scottish children scored an F (the bottom grade) for overall physical activity. In other words, very few Scottish children are meeting the recommended amount of physical activity. Obesity scores are difficult to grade on this system but the report's authors concluded that 6 out of 20 children in Scotland are obese. That means there are 100,000 obese children and young people living in Scotland.

When people are not being physically active they tend to be sitting and now the research into the adverse consequences of being seated for extended periods of time is mounting. Indeed in the USA official agencies are saying that 'sitting is the new smoking' and that prolonged sitting is the number one contributor to chronic diseases.

In the last chapter I quoted Professor Tal Ben Shahar's argument that physical activity is so important to mental health that not taking regular exercise is 'depressing'. I am certain that physical inactivity is one reason why our children are facing mounting mental health problems. Recent research has shown that children as young as four are experiencing anxiety. Suicide and self harm among young people have increased as has the number of children admitted to hospital with eating disorders. One in ten children in the UK has a diagnosed mental illness. One in four girls have depression by the time they are 14.

Reasons why children spend more time indoors and its effects

Various reasons exist why children have been pulled indoors away from nature and from their community. These became evident to me through my own experience of parenthood.

Indoor activities
One of the reasons for this change in behaviour is the imbalance between organised indoor and outdoor activities. When you look around it is easy to observe the many indoor activities organised for children. The list is endless: swimming, Lego, music, gymnastics, playgroups, drama, art, library activities, etc. Most of these activities are needed and, especially when low cost or free, they are hugely beneficial for all of our young people. It's the lack of balance that worries me. As far as I can see there are no, or very few, outdoor weekly activities locally. There are no nature-based groups encouraging children outside. Part of the problem is that people don't see the outdoors as either important or a priority. People think that going outside is a nice thing for children to do but not essential for a good or healthy childhood. This is probably because our culture underestimates the value of playing outdoors or how important nature is to well-being.

Rise in TV and online use
Increasingly children have access to computers, tablets, mobile phones and the internet. Television is also available for 24 hours a day. One third of internet users worldwide are children. Child rights academic Sonia Livingston has updated the United Nations Convention on the Rights of the Child for 'the digital world'. She reports that internet access among 3 to 4-year-olds has increased in one year from 6 hours 48 minutes to 8 hours 18

minutes a week, and 12 to 15-year-olds now spend over 20 hours a week online.

Lack of play spaces

Another problem of childhood is the lack of appropriate spaces to play. If we build on every patch of land there just won't be the opportunity to get children outside. However, this isn't the full story. Many areas have lots of green space, but children aren't using them. This is because getting children outside needs focus and effort. Encouraging children outdoors relies heavily on communities understanding the argument for why children should play outside and the motivation to get them playing outdoors. This is no easy feat since there are so many indoor attractions. There can also be a fatalism about getting children outdoors and a belief that we'll never manage it.

Increase in traffic

Parents often cite fear of children being involved in road accidents as one of the reasons why they don't encourage them to play outdoors. Certainly traffic has increased substantially in recent decades. There is seven times more traffic on the road than there was in 1950 and most of this is private cars. But I'm not convinced this is as important a hurdle as people make out. If it was as simple as this wouldn't there be more campaigns for traffic-free areas and speed restrictions?

Intolerance of children playing

I've heard many people saying that residents in their area aren't very tolerant now of children playing in the street or in local green spaces. Children can be told off for being too noisy or for playing ball games. Decades ago this was much less of a problem as people expected to see children playing outdoors and to see and hear them doing so. There was also a support network in the past whereby neighbours and shopkeepers kept an eye out for the welfare of children playing nearby. This support network made it easier for children to play outdoors.

Parental fears

I remember when my husband and I sent our children to the shops for the first time (aged 5 and 7), it was a nerve-wracking experience for both of us. Like most parents in our society we had been subjected to mass media stories for years about 'stranger danger'. There have always been tragic cases of child murder and abduction and they have been reported in the press. But with the rise of mass media and constant coverage on TV the stories are more prevalent in our lives. It then becomes easy to believe that these tragic incidents are more common than they are. Crime records show that such incidents have not increased. What's more, children are much more at risk within their families and from people known to them than they are with strangers.

All things considered parents are worried about the wrong things. They are unnecessarily anxious about the dangers facing their children outdoors and too blasé about the dangers of the internet. Some of the things children are exposed to online would never be considered appropriate or sanctioned in real life. For example, children are constantly exposed to types of advertising, such as gambling, that wouldn't be permitted in the real world. They also participate online in ways that put them at real risk of being exposed to paedophiles posing as a child and grooming young internet users. Online bullying is a major issue for some young people. Children and young people's deliberate or accidental exposure to internet pornography is also a significant issue. So ironically, in the real world, children are much more protected than in the online world.

The impact of children's disconnection with nature

In the last chapter I presented various arguments and summaries of evidence on the importance of nature for people's mental health. The person who has done most to draw attention to how crucial nature is for children is the American writer Richard Louv. His book *Last Child in the Woods* is an international best seller. He writes:

> For all of human history and of human pre-history, children in their formative years have been going outside and spending much of their time either playing or working in nature. In the matter of two or three decades we are seeing the possible virtual disappearance of that kind of activity in kids.

'Nature deficit disorder' is the phrase Louv coined to explain the impact of losing touch with the natural world. Louv knows that nature deficit disorder is not a known medical diagnosis. You won't find it in any manual of mental or physical disorders. Nonetheless he thinks it a useful way to describe a rising problem – human beings' disconnection from nature, particularly among children, and the negative impact this is having. Louv sets out numerous problems that he thinks nature deficit disorder causes and they are similar to those we encountered in the previous chapter – behaviour and attention problems, obesity, and mood disorders. Louv also argues that if we don't grow up loving nature then we are not likely to look after the natural world properly. He rightly points out that nowadays many adults and children alike 'regard nature as something to watch, to consume, to wear, to ignore'.

Louv worries that there is now a new generation of parents who themselves have grown up without any experience of the natural world. This is an important point when thinking about making change. If we have a generation of parents who haven't experienced – or valued – the natural world themselves then our job in getting their children outside is going to be harder. Therefore it becomes even more important to attempt to change the wider culture to support children and families to be involved in outdoor activity.

Another issue is that as we lose contact with Mother Nature in childhood we also lose the words we need to describe and explain the natural world. In 2007 the Oxford Junior Dictionary for children aged 7 and above took out a number of words like 'moss', 'blackberry' and 'bluebell' to make way for technological terms such as 'blog' and 'chatroom'. In fact 30 words for different species were removed from the dictionary as well as a number of words relating to agriculture. In 2015 28 authors wrote to Oxford University Press asking them to reinstate these natural terms. This then prompted nature writer Robert Macfarlane and illustrator Jackie Morris to produce a beautiful book called *The Lost Words: A Spell Book*. The success of the book took the author and illustrator by surprise. Very quickly a crowdfunding campaign sprung up to raise money to buy books for every Scottish primary school. They succeeded very quickly. Other areas of the UK followed suit. A portion of the proceeds of each book goes to a charity dedicated to empower young people to take action to protect the environment.

If we are to raise children who really care about nature we need to allow, and encourage them, to develop what E. O. Wilson calls 'biophilia' – a love of and connection to the natural world. Nature itself is children's best teacher. Young children develop emotional attachments to what is familiar and comfortable. The more personal experience with nature is, the more environmentally concerned and active children are likely to become.

Resilience and play

As children's outdoor play in nature has declined so too has their resilience. We have come to wrap our children up in cotton wool and protect them from any bad experiences. This protective behaviour comes from a desire to help support our children to grow up safe, happy and healthy. However, the problem with overprotection is that exposure to the normal stresses and strains of life are vital to help build resilience.

In 2018 the distinguished American Positive Psychologist Jonathan Haidt and colleague Greg Lukianoff published a timely book called *The Coddling of the American Mind*. In it they recount numerous current incidents in American campuses whereby students are intent on protecting themselves from anything which they believe will cause them emotional distress. This can be listening to speakers with ideas they dislike or reading books which recount experiences which they find offensive or challenging. 'Microaggression' is the term that is often used. What the current generation of students finds difficult to face simply wasn't an issue for previous generations. And their emotional sensitivity can be seen in the challenging mental health statistics for this cohort of young people.

The authors look at various possible explanations for the different, and overly sensitive, thinking skills of 'iGen' and why they are so vulnerable to mental health problems. Haidt and Lukianoff think it's mainly the result of 'paranoid parenting', a culture of 'safetyism' and a lack of outdoor, independent play. They argue that as all young mammals play, expending energy and putting themselves at risk, it must make an important contribution to development. Indeed they argue that it is 'risky', free play which all children need in order to grow up without unhealthy anxiety and with the skills they require to navigate the adult world. They claim that children's brains require not only 'thousands of hours of play' but also 'thousands of falls, scrapes, conflicts, insults, alliances, betrayals, status competitions, and acts of exclusion' in order to develop. Of course, children need to have healthy attachment and loving relationships with parents, as well as positive friendships, but as they grow they also need to learn how to navigate conflict.

The emphasis that Haidt and Lukianoff place on unsupervised, free play suggests that it is often outdoors but they don't specifically say this and like many psychologists seem oblivious to the importance of being in a green environment. When we combine the benefits of play with the benefits of children being outdoors in nature then we grasp how important wild spaces are for our children's development.

Strategy for playing outdoors and in the local community

Playing outdoors has many benefits for children and for communities:

■ It's fun – and because of this it reduces stress and promotes curiosity and physical activity.

■ It improves mental, social and emotional well-being – by increasing confidence and self-esteem.

■ It builds physical health – through being active outdoors.

■ It brings communities together – through children's presence in the community

■ It supports learning and development – improves attention and creativity.

■ It builds immunity – through exposure to healthy germs.

From the very beginning I believed that children were key to us protecting our Dear Wild Place and that's why we carried out our activities under the banner of the Children's Wood. Here I outline in more detail what we did.

Getting people onto the land

In the Introduction I explained that a major part of our strategy was to get people onto the land. I also outlined there how so much of this was about involving children and those working with them and, of course, parents. I initially did this by starting up an outdoor playgroup and organising weekly, and then monthly, events. I linked up with the local schools and promoted our events with flyers for parents. I tried to get press interest in what we were doing and found it quite easy. For example, we were in a case study for 'Grounds for Learning'. There was an article about us in the 'Early Years Scotland' magazine and then latterly *The Times* newspaper. We had a lucky win early on in the campaign when I got in touch with the writer Julia Donaldson's publicist asking for her support for the space for children to play outdoors. She gave us a quote. We were then able to use *The Gruffalo* and other Julia Donaldson books to promote our activities.

I felt strongly that the Children's Wood could lead by example, and for the first few years I made sure I was the first person there at any event and the last person to leave. To ensure we had everything set up and tidied away I took 100 per cent responsibility for the events including clearing up dog mess and removing any other potentially dangerous items. But increasingly people were happy to help and be involved. This was important but it was not sustainable as it takes time and energy to coordinate volunteers and organise events. It was only three years ago when we started to employ people that our sustainability increased. Our staff now included Andrea Fisher and Jason Byles – two positions for community engagement and land maintenance funded by The Robertson Trust. We now had three times the motivation for getting children and the community more involved. They, like me, took 100 per cent responsibility for events. Since then we've even more involvement from the wider community for supporting children playing outdoors.

Facilitating play outside

To make change and get people outside onto the land we need to make it attractive to people to access their local green space. In January 2012, I arranged for a tree to be cut up into stumps and dug into the ground to create a stepping stone trail. Local residents and friends helped with this. Shortly after we teamed up with The Conservation Volunteers and they brought corporate groups to the land to help us build things to facilitate play: a tipi, mud kitchen, sensory garden and a circle made out of logs for a space to gather. These are still on the land though the mud kitchen has been upgraded and fixed over the years. Recently the CBBC show Junk Rescue has donated a mud kitchen to add to ours. These play things are used day and night by the community at playgroup, schools sessions or just when people come to play on the land.

Local resident and friend Susie Marshall who was also a local teacher at the time, recounts passing through the land and observing some 8 or 9-year-old children at the mud kitchen and they were 'making tea fir the Queen'. Susie said it was brilliant to watch as one of the children had really taken on the responsibility of entertaining the Queen. The mud kitchen is there all the time and children enjoy coming to play on it at any time of the day. Sometimes at the end of the day I'll take my children to the land and they will make me 'dinner'! It's creative work and very rewarding to watch.

Providing evidence of the benefits

To convince people about the importance of getting children outdoors I initially started up a website and Facebook page called 'Enough's Enough, Ditch the Stuff'. This aimed to educate people about the problems of materialism in the lives of children, how this was preventing them from getting outdoors. I then created our Children's Wood Facebook page to talk more widely about the land and other issues related to modern culture and how the land could address these problems. This, and Twitter, allowed us to share evidence and articles around mental health, outdoor learning and the benefits of nature for children and the community. Over the years more people have become involved in our use of social media and as people have come to understand the arguments they have wanted to share information.

Training

I was also aware that we needed to increase people's skills for getting outdoors and pursuing activities. To increase a 'can-do' attitude about being outside I organised various educational events: how to light a fire, plant, build a den, make bows and arrows, cook outdoors and so on. Our intention was to increase the skills within the community. We believed this would not only increase people's connection to the land but also enhance their skills and respect for using and looking after the land.

At the Centre for Confidence and Well-being I had learned about the Forest School movement and so one of the first things

I did when starting the Children's Wood was to find Forest School practitioners nearby. This led me to Mike Brady, the Ghillie Dhu group, and other outdoor learning leaders such as Joyce Macfarlane. They led events for us but I wanted us to have more skills ourselves and ownership of our activities. Subsequently I initiated Forest School training for ten of our volunteers with a view to us running and leading our own weekly club on the land. We started a Saturday club with the aim of applying Forest School principles within the wider community. I thought that this would help people trained in Forest School to share knowledge with others. This would increase skills in others without them having to be trained in the same way. It took us a while to raise the funds and to train everyone but we did it eventually. And we have continued to run the co-operative Saturday morning club thanks to having paid staff to focus on facilitating this and sharing skills with our volunteers.

Overcoming barriers

One of the biggest barriers to people wanting to go to the land and see it as suitable for children playing was dog fouling and in the early days of my involvement there used to be so much dog mess. I remember regularly picking up 30 to 40 dog fouls before we led any child related activity on the land. This was what we needed to do for the first two years or so. The dog mess resulted from one or two antisocial dog walkers; it only takes one person to not pick up dog mess for fouling to become a major issue. Nowadays it is rare to find dog mess on the land despite our large dog-walking community. Dog owners take care and pick up, even when it's not their own dog's mess. So now dog walkers play a very important role on the land, almost like a neighbourhood watch scheme.

A second barrier was that as many children had rarely played outdoors before, they and their parents found it somewhat scary and frightening. In my experience it takes a while to shift this attitude because it's so deeply embedded. During the first year of the Children's Wood I observed the responses of some parents, teachers, assistants and other adults who came for their first experiences at the woodland for outdoor learning and fun. They were very often scared of, unsure of, or unconfident in this semi-wild space. For example, one parent who came with a group from a local nursery school followed her child around the land making sure he didn't fall in a puddle, get muddy or run around. She had no idea that children need to have these experiences. Even uncomfortable episodes such as getting wet can be stimulants for growth and development. Once the child could relax outdoors and the mother give her child space then were able to play and enjoy themselves. But it wasn't this fearful mother's fault that she felt that way. We are constantly subjected to media stories suggesting that paedophiles are around every corner or that children are fragile and at risk of being broken or damaged when playing outside. However, the truth is that children are more at risk of paedophilia online. And, given the importance of play and being in nature, their well-being is much more at risk from not experiencing such activities. ☐

CHAPTER FOUR
Learning outdoors

The necessity for us to maintain contact with the
natural world is essential to the human spirit, yet a
gradual disconnection between children and nature is
occurring. Unfortunately, for many children, school
grounds are one of the only spaces they have access to
for this kind of engagement. If schools sacrifice their
outdoor spaces by expanding their buildings to
manage an increase in pupils, this will certainly
contribute to our children's disconnection with nature.

David Attenborough

THERE are some brilliant strategies and policies put forward by
local councils and the Scottish Government promoting the need
for outdoor learning. However, when I began to be interested
in the topic I was frustrated by the lack of real action in my
area. The thing that most struck me about schooling was the
lack of outdoor play. I thought this was simply part of the bigger
issue of children being absent from our communities. Even in
the early years, where it's possibly easier to implement outdoor
learning, children weren't getting outside enough. I had first
hand experience of this having worked in many nursery schools
across Glasgow. Outdoor learning was not part of, or featured
very low, in the everyday experience of children. Even here there
was a lot of talk about outdoor learning but little actually
happening.

Sometimes schools had an issue accessing nature because they
had very small or concrete playgrounds. This was an important
barrier in our area. I believed that our Dear Wild Place could

help solve this problem. I set up the Children's Wood campaign as I wanted to directly target nursery, primary and secondary schools to get their children learning outdoors. I originally thought there were 14 schools and nurseries that could access the Children's Wood but as time went on and I met more schools the number increased to 22 and we have many more schools from further afield wanting to come and use the land for outdoor learning.

In this chapter I explain why I feel so passionately about learning and playing outdoors and what we did to help those working with children to make this a reality.

What's wrong with education

Our education system is not working for many of our children. In 2016 Scottish schools recorded their worst ever performance in an international survey – the Programme for International Student Assessment (Pisa). Scottish pupils' performance had declined for maths, reading and science. Scots have always prided themselves on their country's educational standards but our performance is now mediocre.

Scotland also has a very pronounced attainment gap between the children who come from affluent families and those living in areas of deprivation. At aged 5 the attainment gap for children from low-income and high-income families is between 10 and 13 months. Lower attainment in literacy and numeracy for children from deprived backgrounds can be seen throughout primary school. Children from deprived households also leave school earlier and many have poor employment outcomes throughout their lives.

The 2016 'Behaviour in Scottish Schools' report asked teachers why there was an increase in low level behaviour problems in schools such as making unnecessary noise, disturbing other workers and work avoidance. Teachers attributed this increase to societal changes (such as the rise in digital technologies), changes in parenting style and the reduction in classroom support for children with additional support needs. Primary school support staff also reported a slight rise in verbal abuse, physical aggression and violent behaviour towards them.

The fact that school isn't working for many of our children is not the teachers' fault. It is the system that is responsible and the wider societal culture. One of these problems is that Scottish children start school aged 5, and sometimes 4. This is becoming a topical issue partly as a result of the Scottish Government's introduction of tests for children in Primary One. Opponents argue that this is leading teachers to 'teach to the test' thus leading to even more formal teaching of 4 and 5-year-olds. Many teachers report that the tests are stressful for many of their young pupils. What's more, if you look at countries which do very well educationally there is no testing until secondary school. In Finland they don't test until the end of secondary school.

So all things considered Scotland could benefit from significantly changing its approach to education. Introducing a kindergarten phase until children are 7 would seem like a good place to start particularly as this would involve lots of outdoor play. The evidence for the impact of nature on children's learning and development is robust – getting outside can help children focus, improve thinking skills and motivation and improve the way they see themselves. Outdoor learning can also de-stress teachers and build relationships and connections.

So all of these types of arguments motivated me to contact schools to see if they would like to use our Dear Wild Place. This was particularly important for schools in our area as many had small or concrete playgrounds. Many of the children lived in flats and didn't have daily access to the outdoors.

The rhetoric and reality of outdoor learning in Scotland

Luckily I was not a lone voice advocating getting school children outdoors. Politicians had been supporting the idea for years and had policies and strategies recognising the need for outdoor learning. This meant that it was easier to argue for why our local schools and communities should be doing it.

At the time, Glasgow City Council had published a report called 'Outside Now' which they hoped would inspire everyone in Glasgow to get outdoors. The strategy aimed to 'benefit every child and young person and raise attainment and achievement'. Maureen McKenna, Executive Director of Education claimed that this is a 'whole society approach to outdoor learning'. Likewise the Scottish Forestry Commission's 'Woods for Learning' strategy, supported by the Scottish Government, emphasised the importance of having areas where children can learn in woodland settings. It also recognised that it was important for these to be within easy walking distance of where many of them live. In their foreword to the strategy Roseanna Cunningham, Minister for the Environment, and Adam Ingram, Minister for Children and Early Learning, state:

> Traditional ideas about classroom teaching are giving way to new and exciting approaches, like the use of woods for learning. Woodlands provide a rich resource for a range of learning opportunities that

can help deliver Curriculum for Excellence. They provide a unique environment for young people to learn about sustainable development.

Those involved in developing Curriculum for Excellence itself have also published a document detailing how it can be delivered through outdoor learning. In it they say that 'progressive and sustainable outdoor learning opportunities are embedded in the new curriculum.'

So there's no doubt that the political and institutional will for outdoor learning is there, but I know from my own observations and from talking to parents and teachers that school children in Scotland are not having these types of experiences everyday. Despite all the political rhetoric, outdoor learning within schools is not a priority.

I also believe that children are suffering from this lack of outdoor time and that it is affecting children unequally. Children from more affluent backgrounds are able to access nature as their families can afford to visit the countryside and holiday in nature. This often isn't an option for those with a low income. Schools can help level the ground by using local spaces for outdoor learning so that children can get outside more.

But why is there a discrepancy between what the policies and documents say about outdoor learning and what's actually happening? I think there are four main reasons why it's hard for schools to implement outdoor learning:

■ Most teachers are not trained in outdoor learning and therefore not confident about using the outdoors for education. Currently both Glasgow University and Strathclyde University Education Departments only have outdoor learning as an elective subject – not as a core part of the training for teachers.

■ It is commonly assumed that there is a lack of outdoor spaces for teachers to use for outdoor learning with their pupils.

■ There is too much fear of potential risks and red tape involved in getting children outside. This puts teachers and schools off taking their children outdoors.

■ Parents complain if their children are outdoors in bad weather or if their child experiences any kind of adversity.

What we did

Given the barriers to outdoor learning I thought it would be helpful to convince schools of the benefits and why it made sense for them to make the effort. I particularly wanted to present senior management in schools with the academic evidence on why outdoor learning is so important to children and young people. So I wrote a paper detailing how learning outside in nature could help children learn better and also feel good. I took this to a few of the local schools and nurseries. In it I detailed the benefit of nature from an educational point of view including, Attention Restorative Theory, Nature Intelligence, evidence for the impact of Forest Schools and Loose Parts Play theory.

I wanted to make it clear to schools that being outside was about more than fun: it is educationally important and can have an impact on learning back at school. I thought that having knowledge or being aware of the educational argument about why nature is beneficial was important in building trust in what we were offering the schools at the Wood and Meadow.

But I soon knew that it wasn't enough just to tell them about the Wood and what it meant for learning. Since outdoor learning was not established or carried out in most local schools they didn't start immediately using the Wood on their own. We had to make it easier for schools to use the land – at least initially. So I contacted and met with the head teachers or senior management team of local schools and we worked out a rota for them to come to the land at times when I would be there to support them.

I also went to the schools and walked classes to the Wood. This had the benefit of teaching staff and children how to get there and increased the chance of them coming. For the first few years, until we started to employ people, I continued to meet with various schools, working out dates with senior management for classes to come to the wood. At the meetings we worked out what the schools wanted and tried to fit our sessions into their curriculum plan – bug hunting, treasure hunts, planting, Halloween, Christmas. We did creative writing sessions, connecting themes to the land and passing on certificates to those who participated. Often the activities we led with the schools would link to the community events happening that month. My thinking was that if we could link the yearly programme of activities in the Wood and Meadow to what the schools were doing then this would help people to think 'community' and 'outdoors'.

One of my strongest memories of these early sessions at the Wood involved a local 9-year-old pupil. He told me that he had never played outside before!! 'Really?' I said. 'Yes,' he answered. I asked him what he would do instead and he replied 'playing computer games with friends'. How could this child never have played outside? Surely not! It made me think the problem was actually worse than I had initially thought. Sadly, he was not the only one who came out with stories like this. Another child said that this was the first time he had been outside to play this year. . . and it was June! Another said he had only ever played in a formal play park, never in a wild space or even out on the street. There were many more stories of this kind when the Children's Wood began.

But the overwhelmingly positive message from the children was that they LOVED it. I also met with teachers who were surprised by certain pupils, particularly those who are silent or quiet in class as they turned into leaders and chatterboxes outside. This supports another branch of research which shows that the outdoors supports child-initiated interactions. Children are more likely to communicate and connect when outdoors.

There's little doubt that there was considerable opposition to what we were doing. Many people opposed the idea of children coming to the space for outdoor learning. One teacher said it was unsafe for children – that same teacher is now involved and is a supporter of the Children's Wood. There were a lot of minds to change and I thought the best way to do this was by continued and regular sessions so that people could experience the land themselves and see what it can do for them, their children and families.

Some research supporting outdoor learning

There is now robust research evidence on the value of getting children outside for learning. Some of this comes from 'Attention Restorative Theory' (ART) which I outlined briefly in Chapter Two. Its main relevance to teachers and educators is that attention can get fatigued from the mental effort required during the school day, and that this can undermine the learning process. This also applies to us as adults and we are often aware that our attention dips in the afternoon. This is because it has taken mental effort to focus on work all morning. Tasks like writing reports or mathematics tire out our thinking skills because they require concentration. The way to restore this 'direct' attention according to ART is to meditate or spend time in nature. Even just spending ten minutes in a green space can recharge direct attention since it engages our more 'indirect' and involuntary attention mechanisms and recharges direct attention. In a nutshell, children who spend time in nature will be calmer and more ready to learn.

The claims for the restorative affect of the outdoors on children is well supported. Two major Swedish studies looked at the difference between an outdoor nursery and a traditional indoors nursery. The first study found that the outdoor group showed better concentration and motor skills. The authors write: 'When it comes to concentration capacity, the children . . . are more than twice as focused as children within a normal pre-school. Their motor skills are better, they are less frustrated, restless and sick.' And teachers had to intervene less in disputes and felt happier about how well they were doing their job.

The second study looked at children's access to outdoor space during nursery time. They compared two groups: one group had restricted access to the outdoors and the second group had at least two hours of access per day. What they found was that children accessing the outdoors more often displayed better co-ordination, balance and agility skills. The researchers believed that the uneven surfaces and trees were behind these improvements.

Forest School

I also highlighted the Forest School approach when talking to teachers. Outdoor and Woodland Learning Scotland describe this as 'an inspirational process that offers children, young people and adults regular opportunities to achieve and develop confidence through hands-on learning in a woodland environment.'

The Forest School idea originated in Scandinavia in the early 1950s. The main idea behind it was to teach children about the natural world. The concept was introduced into the UK in 1995 by a group of early years practitioners who had visited and observed children attending a Forest School in Denmark. Since then it has really taken off in Scotland and the UK in general. Various Forest School courses are running across the country. The Forest School concept has become widely recognised as a good tool for learning which can have a positive effect on children's self-esteem and confidence. A core belief of Forest School practitioners is that it provides a holistic learning environment for the child which aids the development of a positive child/teacher learning relationship characterised by love for the child. The child becomes confident in learning and observes and learns through watching nature.

Forest School is a play and place based experience. It provides children with the freedom to explore and use their creativity. It gives children a multisensory experience which is proven to improve motor skills, focus and concentration. Play outdoors encourages the child to use all of his or her senses and this is fundamental to healthy development. I didn't include play in my original paper for teachers as I thought they would know all this but they didn't. Play, particularly outdoor and unstructured, is so fundamentally important to children as it helps the development of the whole child – psychosocial, social and physical needs. It also teaches skills. As the World Economic Forum observed: 'To be a superhero is to lead; to host a teddy for tea is to organise; to build a fort is to innovate: to play is to learn.'

Place is another important aspect of a Forest School as the child develops a long-term connection with nature through continued exposure to the same setting. They develop a sense of ownership and a desire to protect and take care of the natural world. Having a local green space can connect children to nature and help to build empathy.

Forest School also uses different teaching methods from traditional schools. In a Forest School the child plays an active role in determining what they learn. The Forest School leader facilitates the learning but the child has more control over deciding what they wish to learn. The class sizes are small, usually under twelve, working with the same children over a number of weeks. Learning happens outside in nature, usually in a woodland setting. Children engage with activities like shelter and den building, environmental art, tool use, fire lighting, and nature-based learning and activities.

Nature smart

Another holistic theory I brought to the attention of teachers is Howard Gardner's theory of 'multiple intelligences'. His research, first published in 1983, revealed that children have different types of intelligence and he argued that teachers should be nurturing these different intelligences.

'Nature intelligence' wasn't originally on Gardner's list but he added 'naturalist' or 'nature smart' in 1997 arguing 'the evidence for the existence of a naturalist intelligence is surprisingly persuasive (and). . . it scores well.' Naturalist intelligence includes the ability to nurture and grow things, having a sensitivity to nature and the child understanding their place within it, identifying and distinguishing one species from another, and being able to distinguish diversity of organisms in particular categories.

The implication of Gardner's research is that outdoor learning is of importance when thinking about inclusion. Children have different needs within the classroom and being outside is an essential part of the curriculum. Teaching outside will help teachers to use the natural world to accommodate the naturalist within each child. Gardner also argued that nurturing nature intelligence can support the potential future careers of scientists, naturalists, conservationists, gardeners, farmers and so on.

Loose parts play

Another powerful play tool for increasing children's motivation to engage and learn about the world is what's called 'loose parts play'. In short, playing with different types of materials. This is an idea first put forward in a now famous paper in 1971 by Simon Nicholson, an English architect. Loose parts can be natural objects or things that people have thrown away such as car tyres, material, pallets, crates, kitchen utensils, balls, guttering, bricks and so on. The idea is that children are allowed to do what they like with the items – make a boat, spaceship, village, car etc. The evidence supports the wide-ranging benefits of loose parts play, from increased levels of creative and imaginative play, and improved communication and negotiation skills. When using loose parts children socialise more and are more active. If you've ever watched children engaging in loose parts play in a school playground you'll see how inclusive the activity is. One of our local schools, Dunard Primary School, has introduced loose parts play with great effect. Often football dominates in school playgrounds, but when loose parts are out all children work together creating games and playing. Suddenly the sporty/non sporty, boys/girls divide is reduced and there is more harmony and equality in the playground. In their 2015 book on the topic Daly and Beloglovsky write:

> When children interact with loose parts, they enter a
> world of 'what if' that promotes the type of thinking
> that leads to problem solving and theoretical
> reasoning. Loose parts enhance children's ability to
> think imaginatively and see solutions, and they bring a
> sense of adventure and excitement to children's play.

The woodland itself is a playground for loose parts: twigs, leaves, undulating ground, bushes, logs, fallen trees and so on. However, in our small heavily used woodland where the planting is quite young it was necessary to introduce other loose parts. A local dad, Jeff, left some guttering a few years ago and we still bring this out at playgroup and add balls to make fun games. Often local people bring items to us or we take items like guttering from skips or ask builders for donations. We have developed our loose parts play and facilitate their use at our playgroup and school sessions in creative ways.

Empowering teachers

To empower our teachers locally we decided to start an education committee to help focus on activities that teachers and other educators could do with children and young people outdoors. This led to us developing education packs with activities and ideas that linked to the Curriculum for Excellence and that local teachers – or those from further afield – could use outdoors. This started off with just one-off activities and has developed into whole packs. We also organised training for local teachers in some basic skills for using the outdoors such as 'how to tie knots', 'how to risk assess outdoors' and 'how to encourage children's imagination'.

Disengaged or disaffected young people

More recently we have been working with a 'hard to reach' group of young people who form a gang in our area. Their antisocial behaviour means that this particular group is known to residents and schools as well as Police Scotland, Tesco, McDonalds and local shops. Through our evening youth work we have got to know these young people well and have developed a trusting relationship with them. What we have found out is that many of this group come from very challenging family backgrounds. There is a lot of interest in Adverse Childhood Experiences (ACEs) nowadays and many in this group would score highly. For those who aren't familiar with this terminology it means exposure in childhood and adolescence in the home to such things as a parent committing suicide or having mental health problems; a parent misusing alcohol or drugs; or witnessing domestic violence. ACEs also include the child's own experience of sexual, emotional or physical abuse. These, and other ACEs, can be traumatic for young people. The ACE research shows that the more people encounter these type of events at home the more stressed they are likely to be. This type of stress in childhood can undermine long term physical and mental health and lead to addictions. Children and adolescents displaying challenging behaviour are often the ones who have suffered most.

But these weren't the only type of challenges these young people were suffering from. Boredom was also a factor. There is nothing free for them to do outwith school apart from hang around. When they are in school they are usually there for only 20 per cent of the time, and leave by lunchtime. They can also be very disruptive. In one incident the school had to shut down for 45 minutes because of behaviour issues.

Given their disengagement from school it is easy to see why many of this group hate school and leave without formal qualifications. School constantly makes them feel bad about themselves because they can't do the work. What's more, as a result of childhood trauma and stress, many can't control their emotional responses and end up doing something that lands them in a room alone or in detention.

Given what's happened to so many of these youngsters I feel that they are being so badly let down by the system and believe that we could be doing so much more for this group. The question we need to ask is: How can we make compulsory education more meaningful, purposeful and developmental for this group of young people so that they can achieve something worthwhile?

I believe that green spaces like our Dear Wild Place have a role. We have begun to target young people in this group who we can see are the leaders or influencers. We believe that if we could turn their behaviour around and support them in being positive role models in their group then change will happen.

Because we were already working in the evenings with this group, I wanted to extend our work to encompass the school day. This would allow us to take a more holistic approach and build our connection with them. I approached two local secondary schools and together we identified six young people from our local gang who we could work with. We got funding from Glasgow City Council and asked Venture Scotland to lead a tailored programme. It involved canoeing, climbing, hillwalking and mountain biking. The youngsters will eventually receive an SVQ award for their involvement.

Through this work young people are getting to know themselves. They really enjoy the days and think the programme 'cool'. Importantly it is a positive experience for a group used to remedial classes, detention, and time-out zones. This is a project where they are developing skills that will help them throughout life: communication, group work and confidence. They feel proud of what they are doing. This is the first time Venture Scotland have worked with this age group and already they can see the power of this type of programme for these young people.

There are other boys we are working with. We take them out weekly into the Wood and Meadow and get them involved in different outdoor activities. I believe that if we can bring these young people outdoors more they will come to see learning as something meaningful and purposeful and it will encourage them to feel that they are growing and developing. We are planning to provide opportunities for young people to learn bushcraft, Forest School, gardening and other skills that might provide them with a different pathway in life. We also find out what our young people want to do and help them do it. This can be fixing bikes, dancing, or parkour, as there is mounting interest in this. But most of all we hope that the land can provide respite and relaxation for many of these youngsters who have high levels of anxiety in their day-to-day lives. One particularly successful day was when we took the group fishing. They caught a trout then brought it back to the land where they gutted, cleaned, cooked and ate the fish.

Probably one of the most rewarding moments for me since we started our youth work concerns a young person, aged 10 at the time, who is often hypervigilant (constantly on the look out for danger). He is aggressive and badly behaved in school where teachers find it difficult to support his needs. If he goes to school at all, he very rarely stays beyond the morning break. Indeed his teacher told me that in school he is almost impossible to work with. However, when he's on the land this same boy is well behaved and I have never seen his aggressive side. One day when I was on the land with the boy he told me, 'I feel relaxed here'. Another day when I was on the land celebrating my daughter's seventh birthday the same boy turned up and we asked him to join us. He happily played hide and seek, tag and other games with us. He was like any other child his age – a complete contrast to the times when he threw a brick through a car window or attacked another schoolmate. This boy needs to play and relax in a natural environment where he feels safe.

All this might seem trivial but the fact that being in our Dear Wild Place made this boy feel relaxed made all our work worthwhile. This boy is experiencing adversity, he is scared most of the time and his long-term future is not looking good. For him to say that he feels relaxed was profound. It was proof for me that nature has the power to help people and the value of community green spaces.

Future teachers

If we are to get teachers to embrace outdoor learning then they need to be trained properly. When Monica Porciani from Strathclyde University got in touch with us to ask if students in the elective module, 'Learning for Sustainability', could come to the Meadow and Wood for a placement we jumped at the chance. The placements have been very successful and we are now in our fourth year of collaborating with the students. Monica Porciani has been very positive about what we have to offer saying that 'The Children's Wood was the only local community organisation which we were able to identify and which was positioned to offer our students this opportunity and help in their professional development.' She thinks it important that her students 'were also able to experience free play and learning in a natural environment – an experience which we currently find difficult and almost impossible to provide for student teachers.' The fact that the pupils who come to the Children's Wood are from a wide range of backgrounds and have different support needs was another bonus for the students. For all these reasons Monica Porciani believe that the Children's Wood is 'a unique resource on our doorstep.'

The challenges

We must be aware that political aspirations to make learning outdoors part of all children's everyday educational experience are not being realised. And they won't be unless all schools and nurseries can access a safe local space like the Children's Wood and Meadow. This is vital and why I am arguing for the use of derelict and vacant local wild spaces to be upcycled to encourage outdoor learning. What we've achieved with the Children's

Wood could happen in other areas. We hope it does happen elsewhere. We have schools visiting and enquiring from across the city from areas such as Sighthill, Knightswood and the city centre. If these places had a local patch of land to use it would cut down on buses, overuse of our site, and the development of biodiversity, play and community in these other local areas.

When thinking about getting children outside for learning, it's important to look around at the potential spaces available in your community. All of our events started off as guerrilla children's activities as they were a bit like guerrilla gardening whereby people start planting seeds on disused land so that the area becomes more pleasant and nurturing. We went to huge efforts not just to risk assess but also remove any dog mess, rubbish and so on to make people feel safe and to ensure children were protected from any real dangers.

You need very little to get started. I started the Children's Wood with nothing, except for some ideas and a vision and support from a couple of close friends and my husband. Very quickly people got on board and with projects like this people are willing to get involved. Yes it has been challenging at times but the feedback from those now using the land always makes it worthwhile as can be seen in this quote from a local head-teacher:

> The availability of a woodland setting immediately accessible to our children and staff, on the doorstep of the school, is a real living experience. This natural beautiful and exciting environment is alien to many city centre children and is impossible for schools to replicate in their playground as it has taken decades to evolve naturally – a real wood. ☐

CHAPTER FIVE

Community matters

This is such a great inner city open space, a real 'secret garden' which serves as an open-air community centre.
                                                    Julia Donaldson

COMMUNITY values have been declining over the past decades. The UK has been labelled the loneliest country in Europe and people feel less connected to their neighbours than ever before. At the same time there are many problems facing communities such as inequality, poverty, mental and physical health issues and troubled children and adolescents. These issues are getting progressively worse for communities and agencies, like the NHS, are struggling to cope. It is clear that we need to think about alternative ways to address local needs and I believe communities themselves can do this. Communities used to be stronger and people were more connected and able to work together. A connected community can fix and prevent problems.

When I began the Children's Wood I wanted to actively build community feeling by involving people in defending our patch of land from the threat of development. I also viewed our land as a place to commune with each other, an outdoor community centre, a modern day church without the religion, and a town square without the shops. In short I saw it as a place where people can gather together informally and formally and connect with one another.

It might be worth saying something about how I see our local community. For me it is a group of people connected to each other through the Meadow and Wood, or the projects local people have initiated that are connected to this outdoor space. I also see our community initiatives as:

- local people creating regular events and opportunities for others to get involved with on the land or in the local area

- led by local people

- meeting the needs of local people

- solving problems in a makeshift or 'do it yourself' kind of way

- creating an atmosphere or ethos that is inclusive, welcoming, caring and empowering

- there if you want it.

In this book I mainly refer to community in a geographical way. But I'm also aware that we have people who live as far away as Dunoon or even Canada who still feel part of our community so it's not just about local community. Sometimes community refers to a group of people who share and pursue similar values. The Children's Wood and North Kelvin Meadow have encouraged lots of people to support or identify with our community because we articulate values they share on the type of society we want to create.

The decline of community

Bowling Alone by Robert Putnam became an international bestseller when it was first published almost twenty years ago. In it Putnam warned his fellow Americans that their 'social capital' was declining and that this was having a profoundly negative effect on individuals' lives and on communities. He paints a bleak picture of people not knowing neighbours, having fewer friends, belonging to fewer organisations and clubs and even signing fewer petitions. Putnam outlines a variety of factors which are making modern life more individualistic and less conducive to community. One is the decline of outdoor play. Putnam argues that playing outside was an important part of social capital because children who played together became friends. Then parents and the local community got to know each other, neighbours took part in group activities, and they shared things. In this way wider community bonds were formed. For Putnam the move away from outdoors to indoors has seriously impacted civic life and our overall health and well-being.

This shift from outdoor to indoor life, from community to individualism, is in part due to the rise of television. Indeed researchers in the USA have shown that as television came into people's lives their involvement in community organisations plummeted. This is why Putnam argues that the easiest way for people to build community is 'to turn off the TV' as 'the more entertainment television you watch, the less civically engaged you are. People watch *Friends* rather than having friends.' When we add in the lure of computers and social media it is easy to understand why people have become isolated and why we have fewer active communities.

As society has become less civic minded and more individualistic loneliness has risen. Loneliness is now a serious public health issue. In fact social isolation is as bad for your health as smoking 15 cigarettes per day. Loneliness is worse for health than obesity, and lonely people are more likely to suffer from heart disease, depression and dementia.

The Office for National Statistics (ONS) has found that in Britain people are less likely to know their neighbours or have strong friendships than any other country in the EU. Britain is ranked 26th out of 28th for the percentage of people who say they have someone to turn to if there is a serious problem, and 27th in the rank for feeling close to people in their local area. Only around 50 per cent of British people say they know their community well. In the UK there are 1.2 million chronically lonely older people.

The Campaign to End Loneliness has found that over two thirds of people in Glasgow have experienced loneliness. But loneliness is not only a problem of old age. Other research published by ONS finds that young adults are the loneliest group in the UK: around 10 per cent of young adults say they are 'always' or 'often' lonely. This is a higher percentage than it is for people over 65. A 2010 report by the Mental Health Foundation found that 18-34 year olds in their survey were likely to feel depressed because of loneliness.

It's hard to believe that in an age where we are all connected via the internet through social media apps like Facebook that people could be lonely. But they are. Online relationships are no substitute for the real thing. Having good friends makes you happy and the more friends you have the happier you are, but this only holds true for real life relationships: increasing the number of friends on Facebook doesn't increase happiness.

The societal change outlined above – from outdoor to indoor, community to individualism – reflects a shift in values. Researchers have been tracking values over the last fifty years and what they have found is that our values have shifted from 'intrinsic' to 'extrinsic'. Intrinsic values are goals that are developed around personal growth and include things like connection to community, relationship with family and friends, personal development or spirituality. Extrinsic values are about seeking fame, money image, status or possessions. Decades ago people's top values were intrinsic – for example, friendship, spiritual development or community. But these top values have now flipped and people now value materialist, extrinsic goals.

Professor Tim Kasser has been studying the effect of extrinsic, materialistic values for decades now. His research shows that the more people pursue these values the worse their well-being and mental health. This is true for both adults and children. He argues that one of the best ways to undermine materialist values is to promote intrinsic ones and to encourage people to see how satisfying they can be. Encouraging people to spend time together outdoors promotes intrinsic values. This is why breaking down extrinsic values was a byproduct of our various campaigns.

One of the reasons why extrinsic, materialist values are so dominant, is that they are in tune with what is now called 'Neoliberalism'. This is our current form of free-market capitalism which not only focuses exclusively on economic growth but extends its profit-seeking ideology into the public and private realm. *Guardian* writer George Monbiot maintains that Neoliberalism is 'the ideology at the root of all our problems'.

Because the system Neoliberalism creates is both self-serving and sustainable it's powerful and hard to undermine or override. The problem is that it is profoundly unethical: it has left the poor poorer, increased materialistic values and feelings of unhappiness and loneliness and, by stimulating overconsumption, used up planetary resources. Monbiot argues that Neoliberalism has not simply been economically disastrous but politically as well: politicians of both the right and left have adopted Neoliberal policies and this has led people to become politically disengaged and inactive. It is also why there are so few voices putting forward a radical alternative to this immoral political creed. However, communities can be a good place to start challenging Neoliberal values by adopting more intrinsic values and to start filtering up the change from the grassroots.

Meaning and purpose

One of the great things about community involvement is that it not only can shift people's values, it can also boost people's well-being and positive feelings. And it is not difficult to understand why.

Over the last seven years I have often returned to a book I love called *Man's Search for Meaning* by Viktor Frankl, an Austrian neurologist and psychiatrist. Frankl was a holocaust survivor and his book recounts what he learned living in a concentration camp. He was deeply affected by seeing how some people survived and thrived in the camp despite the terrible circumstances. He goes on to argue that those who survived this terrible ordeal had a strong sense of purpose and meaning in life. 'Those who have a 'why' to live,' he wrote, 'can bear with almost any 'how'.'

One of the leaders of the Positive Psychology movement, Professor Martin Seligman, also argues that meaning is profoundly important to people's well-being. At the Centre for Confidence and Well-being's influential Vanguard Programme held in Glasgow in 2005 Seligman argued that by definition meaning is about 'serving a goal bigger than yourself.' This can be a challenge in our narcissistic, individualistic age when we are repeatedly told that to find happiness we must put ourselves and our wants at the centre of our own lives.

Bearing this in mind I am very much aware that our campaigns have brought a strong sense of meaning and purpose to our community and this has allowed us to overcome some apparently insurmountable obstacles. Having a sense of meaning and purpose is also important when thinking about *how* to get people outside more and to help people to continue coming outside. Any community-based project inevitably faces constant competition with digital devices, as well as media scare stories, which draw people back indoors and away from their communities. A strong sense of meaning and purpose helps people and their community develop a collective aim and this in turns helps to overcome naysayers, risk aversion or fatalism.

Caring

Caring for each other and also for the land is at the heart of the Children's Wood project and no doubt has also improved the well-being of those involved. One of my favourite psychologists, Ellen Langer, has managed to demonstrate the importance of caregiving on something as vital as human longevity. In the mid-1970s she undertook research which found that giving older people living in a care home a plant to look after (as well as more control over other aspects of their lives) increased their lifespan. This simple study demonstrated the health benefit which can result from caring and looking after a living thing.

There is a simple explanation why caring provides a health benefit and it is because caring releases oxytocin, a chemical sometimes nicknamed the 'love hormone' as it is also released in sexual and intimate encounters. Oxytocin promotes maternal attachment to an infant as well as facilitating childbirth and breastfeeding. It is released in all kinds of social relationships, from hugging someone to volunteering. In a nutshell, nurturing relationships increase our oxytocin levels. It is the primary hormone involved in social bonding and promoting trust. Oxytocin provides a calming and relaxing effect. Increased oxytocin has been linked to:

- improved immune system

- less cortisol (a stress hormone)

- longevity

- reduced drug cravings

- improved social skills

- sleep

- generosity

- improved mental health.

Increased oxytocin is thought to improve mental health because it fosters social connectivity. It can decrease stress by increasing the ability to respond to socially relevant stimuli and lowering cortisol levels.

The pleasurable feeling that caring can bring to the carer helps to explain why we were so often aware that people enjoyed volunteering and helping out as well as bringing along various gifts. People's acts of kindness had a positive effect on themselves and not just on others.

Building a community of connected people is about facilitating communication and breaking down barriers that exist between the different groups. In our case it might seem odd or counter-intuitive that dog walkers and children could both use and enjoy the land as they have different needs. However, it works. And it works in part because there are key figures in the different communities who help to forge good relationships with other groups. Much of this is about solving problems through talking. We won a finalist place for the 'My Place Award' from the Civic Trust in 2013, and the judges were surprised when they came to visit by the harmony between the different communities. They wondered how such a multi-use space could be so successful. I believe that people find ways round problems and aren't obsessed by their own group's interests because they have such a strong shared vision for the land. Another reason why people are so committed to our Dear Wild Place is that they can see how it can meet the needs of our wider community.

Meeting the needs of local people – mental health

As mentioned in the chapter on green space, mental health is now a major issue in our society. In Chapter Two I showed how contact with nature and being outdoors can help alleviate depression and help people to feel better. But social interaction and opportunities to care for something or someone are also beneficial to mental health. This means that our Dear Wild Place which offers people the opportunity to be in nature as well as with other people can be hugely beneficial for those suffering from mental ill health or loneliness.

Projects based in the Children's Wood and Meadow deliberately try to combine contact with nature and social interaction.

For example, we run a general gardening club called Growing North Kelvin Meadow, where adults can plan, plant, grow and reap the fruits of their labour. The vegetables grown in the garden are used in community meals. We've found this provides an opportunity for people to connect in a deeper way to the land and to one another. One woman who comes to our gardening club suffers from depression and appreciates the fact that she can drop in and out depending on how she is feeling and that there is no pressure to come every week. She often takes a month or two off and then comes back. This is the beauty of community activities – they are there if you need them.

Alongside the gardening sessions we've just started a mental health programme, designed to boost mental health and well-being. Local GPs and medical centres can refer people, or people can self-refer. At the moment there is some social prescribing in our area but as we expand our weekly mental health programme we anticipate that more doctors will send patients to our group. To do this, we need to link up with local centres and provide them with the details of the sessions to which they can refer patients. We hope that given the pressure the NHS is under, and the side effects of anti-depressants, that what we offer will be attractive to local health providers. One group is a local NHS peer support group and they have enjoyed coming back to see their meadow seeds flowering or vegetables growing. It provides a sense of satisfaction and connection and some of the group have been attending the regular gardening sessions outwith the peer support sessions.

Recently we have collaborated with Dr Kate Reid of Glasgow University. Her students were interested in studying the impact of community spaces on adult mental health. Four different strands of research were carried out between December 2017 and August 2018, by MSc postgraduate students from the Psychological Studies programme. Among other things the unpublished research found that people who had little access to nature scored higher for stress.

Meeting the needs of local people – inequality, stress and play

The Spirit Level: Why equality is better for everyone was first published in the UK in 2009 and had an immediate impact. Its authors, Richard Wilkinson and Kate Pickett, set out compelling arguments for why living in a very unequal society is psychologically damaging for those at the bottom of the pecking order. But they also argued that since inequality erodes trust even the better-off suffer. Their message is significant as it conveys powerfully that the problem with inequality is not just lack of resources or poverty – it is also about how people feel.

I have little doubt that Wilkinson and Pickett's arguments had such a major impact because the UK is one of the most unequal societies in the world. Another thinker who has helped us to see how bad the UK's inequality problem has become is social geographer, Professor Danny Dorling. He shows that from 1919 to the late 1970s year on year Britain became fairer and there was reasonable social mobility. But at the end of the 1970s this changed and we now have levels of inequality which pertained in the UK in the mid-nineteenth century when Charles Dickens wrote *Hard Times*.

Inequality is a huge issue for our project. The site is technically in Maryhill, the 4th most deprived ward in Europe, but it borders Kelvinside one of the most affluent areas in Europe. So in our area there are those who have lots of resources, money and amenities and those who have nothing. From early on in our campaign I wanted to highlight the importance of inequality. One of the things we did was show a documentary, inspired by *The Spirit Level*, called *The Divide* in Maryhill Burgh Halls. The director Katharine Round spoke at this event. The film portrayed the grim reality of income inequality, for people in the UK and America.

I could see the potential of our wild place as a resource, a buffer, for reducing stress and other negative outcomes associated with income inequality. But more importantly I thought that the land could help reduce social barriers and encourage mixing – something which becomes increasingly unlikely in very unequal societies like ours.

The benefit of having local wild spaces for communities experiencing deprivation was further supported by research published in 2013 by the National Children's Bureau. Their report 'Greater Expectations: raising aspirations for our children' looked at the state of childhood and poverty in England. The report compared data from their 1969 landmark study 'Born to Fail' with current figures. People were shocked when the original study was published as it painted a bleak picture as so many children were living in poverty and facing real disadvantage. Sadly the authors state that the picture which emerges from their new research 'shows that far from improving over time, the situation today appears to be no better than it was nearly five decades ago.' They also say that in some respects it is 'worse'.

One of the areas that has got worse is children's access to green space and play spaces. In fact the researchers found that children living in the most deprived areas in the UK are significantly less likely to have access to green space and places to play. The difference is not marginal and it wasn't always like this:

> In 1969 disadvantaged children had the same level of access as their peers to outdoor leisure facilities. However, this is not the case today. Children living in the least deprived areas are nine times more likely than those living in the most deprived areas to enjoy good local environments for play and recreation.

Our project obviously can't do anything about income inequality, though we can publicise how awful it is through events such as *The Divide* film screening. But we certainly can help ameliorate the effects of inequality by encouraging youngsters deprived of nature onto our land and we can also try to encourage social cohesion by encouraging lots of different people in the area to come to events or just hang out in this wild space. There is no need to dress in a particular way or bring money since there is usually nothing to buy (and when we do have home baking it's usually a donation).

We think it is important that many of the schools using the land are in areas where most of the children live in flats with no gardens and never play or spend time in wild spaces. This lack of green space can exacerbate the impact of income inequality because people are losing the calming and resilience-building effects of nature.

Vulnerable children and youth

Through one of our youth groups we work with vulnerable children and young people who are roaming the streets. They are bored, have little money, and are very stressed and vulnerable. Inevitably some of them are in trouble with Police Scotland. Many of these youngsters come from Maryhill and have parents who are drug users. Most have suffered from various traumatic experiences. Their antisocial behaviour makes others feel scared of them and don't want to get involved.

But we have got involved and are giving them opportunities to participate in various activities. We spoke to a new police officer at Maryhill Police station and between us we managed to bring together others in the local area who are also concerned about our young people – McDonalds, Partick Thistle football club, local teachers and community members. Recently we ran a training session with Dr Suzanne Zeedyk on how to use insights on childhood trauma to work better with this group. We have started monthly meetings to discuss how we can best support these vulnerable young people. We are now planning community football matches and over the winter we moved our youth club into McDonalds so we could start working where the young people like to hang out. We are building positive strong relationships between the young people and ourselves and this we believe is the key to supporting them as they grow older, and it will connect them to the wider community. This is starting to make a difference. The young people we have been working with have demonstrated some positive changes like trying to reduce aggressive behaviour in their peers. They are also showing a willingness to help out within the community.

When working with this group it is particularly important to show that you are reliable and consistent. They often ask 'when will this end?' or say things like 'I feel like this is a dream, good things usually feel like a dream.' But reliably putting on activities and showing that you are here to stay allows such vulnerable young people to trust and have hope for a different future.

Meeting local needs – challenging stereotypes

When the Children's Wood first began I was aware that there is a widespread view that it is only certain types of people who get involved in environmental or access-to-nature activities – middle class, left-wing, vegetarian, bohemian. This stereotype can make it hard for other people to engage with environmental issues because they think they don't belong. I was keen to get away from the classic stereotype so that all types of people would also engage and reap the benefits.

I was also aware that the limiting nature of stereotypes is relevant to many different aspects of our community – not just environmentalists but also poor people, adolescents or the elderly. Communities can challenge all of these stereotypes by bringing people together and seeing them as equally important and valued.

In the UK all young people can suffer from the negative stereotype of adolescents. Even a simple thing like young people being outside in groups is an issue for many adults who feel threatened by adolescents. There are even some initiatives within city centres in the UK which seek to deter young people from hanging around. These areas are fitted with machines that make high-pitched sounds, designed only to be heard by teenagers who have more sensitive hearing than adults. The goal is to make the noise so intolerable to young people that it drives them out of these areas.

Do we dislike young people so much that we want to drive them away like this? Initiatives like these also highlighted how far removed young people are from the adult world. The idea behind these initiatives is that *all* teenagers are a problem and therefore we can't have any of them hanging around. They are not welcome. Even if the group of teenagers is a problem, these initiatives don't solve it: they just move the problem into another area.

I have noticed that when groups of young people hang around outdoors, adults tend to think they are up to no good. Even if that group isn't actually doing something 'bad', nonetheless the perception is that there will be trouble. This negative view of young people is limiting and undermining and at times will become a self-fulfilling prophecy.

Some argue that adolescence itself is a creature of our society. In his book *The Case Against Adolescence*. Robert Epstein argues that adolescence, and the problems associated with it, are a man-made phenomenon as it exists mainly in western countries.

There's little doubt that adolescence can be a troubled time. Suicide rates and mental health problems are increasing for this age group. The commonly held view is that the teenage brain develops in such a way that it leads adolescents to act in anti-social ways and to seek out risky experiences. 'The teen brain' theory has led some people to adopt a fatalistic, or even antagonistic, attitude towards young people, not believing that they are responsible or mature. This then leads society to put more restrictions or rules in place to keep teenagers under control. Epstein's research in the US found that: 'Young people are subjected to more than 10 times as many restrictions as are mainstream adults, twice as many restrictions as active-duty U.S. Marines, and even twice as many restrictions as incarcerated felons.' Epstein disputes the idea that there is something inherently wrong with teenagers' brains, arguing that they are much more capable than we give them credit for and in many instances are actually better than adults at certain tasks and skills.

I have also been aware that when it comes to young people connecting with nature or even just being part of the community, there are not many opportunities. Many hobbies, clubs and sports have a cost that can deter young people from becoming involved. The activities that are put on for young people are often planned by a well-intentioned adult or group, but with little or no consultation about what young people really want to do. We then wonder why engagement might be low and blame our young people when they start acting up.

We have started to challenge a conventional approach in our own community by involving young people in our events and getting them to organise and plan what they want to do. We've started a G20 Youth Festival in order to let the young people take control.

With older people, it is worth mentioning the psychologist Ellen Langer again. She carried out another landmark research study on the power of stereotypes and inhibiting beliefs. Langer and fellow researchers got men in their seventies and eighties, divided them into two groups and then took a group at a time to a monastery for a week. The first group were asked to pretend that they were back living in the 1959 and researchers primed the environment to help them act the part: they played music from the period, had a vintage radio, showed black and white films and littered the place with items from the 1950s. The other group were also treated to these experiences but they weren't asked to pretend they were back in the 1959: they were only asked to reminisce about their lives.

Before and after the monastery experiment both groups were given a range of cognitive and physical tests. After just one week there were positive results across the board – hearing, vision, posture, flexibility all improved. So did their performance on intelligence tests. Both groups showed positive results but the men who had been asked to act as if they were back in 1959 showed even more benefits. In a lecture about the research Langer told the audience: 'Wherever you put the mind, the body will follow' and that 'it is not our physical state that limits us, it is our mindset, our perceptions, that draws lines in the sand.' And those perceptions are created by a society with very negative stereotypes about ageing.

Langer's study illustrates the power of belief and how this can shape people's behaviour. Challenging the normative views of ageing (or other things such as weight, race etc) in this way can break down the limitations people place on themselves as a result of societal norms.

Bringing people of all ages together can challenge the often-negative perceptions we have of older people as being slow, ill and housebound or of young people as being reckless and immature. There are quite a number of older people who are involved in the Children's Wood and Meadow. Some of my closest friends who are involved with the Children's Wood are older than me – Anne Whitaker, Ian Halliburton, Ralph Green and Alex Macgregor. What you realise when you spend time with older people is that they don't fit classic stereotypes. They are often just like me only wiser and more experienced.

So the great thing about communities is that they have the power to challenge stereotypes as they can provide opportunities to connect with people of all ages and backgrounds.

Building community

Here are what I see as the essential ingredients in building community:

- Shared values and goals: The value/goal can be stopping a housing development, for example, or running projects to foster equality, mental health, contact with nature, or facilitate intergenerational activities.

- Regular opportunities to get together: We did this through gardening, community gatherings, schools sessions, playgroups, and conservation days.

- Anti perfection: Do things in a makeshift/do-it-yourself kind of way. This gets away from business as usual perfection and increases confidence in others. If you can show someone how easy it is to do something, and not have standards that are too high, it might inspire others to do it too. I have also found it useful to forget things as this is a great way to involve people. For example, if you forget milk then it encourages someone else to offer to get some from their house or nip to the shop. In short, forgetting something can be a great way to involve others.

- Encourage leadership and responsibility: From early on we asked people to lead activities that they weren't likely to volunteer for. Our aim was to get people more involved. If more people took on leadership roles then they would involve more people and take more responsibility. This has a knock-on or ripple effect. Training people also helps people to build up the skills to lead.

- Sometimes doing something is better than doing nothing at all: Often we are put off doing things as we think they have to be properly organised. But often it's good enough to do something even if that means it won't be well planned and executed. A good example is outdoor play. Just getting children outside is good enough, you don't have to do anything too elaborate to reap the benefits.

■ Facilitate ideas: Help community members to achieve what they would like to do. We have helped community members to bring a labrynth to the land, and a beedookit (a community project where bees are housed in a structure like a pigeon dookit). We have also helped people to put on events or lead sessions which interest them.

■ Shared ownership of both spaces and ideas: We celebrate all the different groups on the land and people are actively encouraged to get involved or help out with gardening, land maintenance or events. One grandmother came to the land with her child and she referred to the land as her 'backgarden' I think many people feel the same.

■ Regular events: Our community has pulled together the type of shared events which I have outlined throughout this book.

■ Just start talking: Talk to people in your community. Use every opportunity.

Sustainability

A community needs to be nurtured and supported. Three years ago when we started to employ people we split a part time role in half so we had people to work with schools and encourage wider community engagement. Having paid positions allowed us to do so much more in bringing the community together and onto the land. Since then we have increased the hours and we now have four employees along with many sessional workers who support people in accessing nature and building community. It would be difficult to do what we have done solely with volunteers. These posts, even if they are only a few hours a week, can be great development opportunities for people, and can give a community more capacity to further build community.

Here is a quote from a local young person who is still involved in the land and who we have employed over the years. He wrote this for the Public Hearing outlined in Chapter One:

> I'm here as a 19 year old to talk about how the Meadow has benefited me and others like me. Although I've been living in the area for most of my life, it was only about a year ago that I started to get involved. I'd returned to my parents' flat after a while travelling. I had few friends and was depressed, searching unsuccessfully for work. It was then that I met Jayson, who was doing much of the gardening work around the land. I came down to help him the next day, and before I knew it I was spending several days a week doing gardening work down at the Meadow. I was joined there over the months by various other local youths, including a small core of regular volunteers that Jayson had got involved. All of us were unemployed at the time, and the Meadow gave us a reason to get out of bed, get some company and exercise, and feel like a valuable part of our community.

This young person has gone on to be a significant figure in helping build community as is clear from his statement:

> Since finishing school I've been struggling to choose a career path – the Meadow changed that. My volunteering experiences helped me to secure a work placement in another community garden, and I have now been accepted onto a Horticulture HND course. Since my placement ended I've had some paid work

for the Children's Wood, organising community events and upholding the land. This is my first position of such responsibility, and I am extremely grateful to the Children's Wood for opening this opportunity up to me. ☐

CHAPTER SIX

Running a successful campaign

It is often easier to ask for forgiveness
than to ask for permission.

Grace Hopper

DO YOU want to stop a housing development or convince authority figures of the value of derelict or vacant land? Then I would suggest taking an indirect approach to building community and creating a living alternative. I don't think it's always enough to argue about the potential of a piece of land or the benefit of having green space locally if there isn't wider engagement with the space and an idea of how this can be sustainable. Showing another way to do things demonstrates that you are serious, that you have something real rather than just an interesting concept or an idea that may never materialise or last. What's more, an initiative that meets local needs can galvanise the community around something to fight for. This can also provide hope and optimism because it helps people to see that problems are solvable, and counteracts fatalism.

This is what we did. We galvanised people around land and how it could address needs such as the education gap, material-ism, children's mental and physical health, inequality, loneliness and environmental issues. People got actively involved in both saving the land but also in addressing these major issues locally.

Our campaign to save the North Kelvin Meadow from a housing development, enhanced, interacted with, and sometimes just got in the way of building community and addressing needs. It's hard to separate out the two things because they were interlinked, and grew together. Both helped each other in their development and ultimate success.

In this chapter I highlight a few things that helped our campaign to save the land.

The facts

When the Children's Wood started I knew we had a good solid argument and this was partly due to the previous efforts of local people such as Phil Nicholson, Gordon Barnes, Kate Wooding, Andy Whyte, Dragana Whyte, Douglas Peacock and my husband Quintin Cutts. The Council were clearly going against planning policies. However, I thought that an argument wasn't enough, since we all know how often planning decisions can be unfair and the little person often loses out. We wanted to create a visceral heart-felt campaign. We needed more support and backing from other people since we would need people power to win this. This allowed us to build on existing arguments and create new ones.

An alternative

I have argued throughout this book that I thought our land could meet some of the twenty-first century needs within our community and we set to work trying to demonstrate this through community events, gardening clubs, schools and playgroups. We needed to reach the whole community. This was everyone's land and we wanted to invite people on to it to experience it and get involved. We acted as if our lives depended on it, since we never knew when the planning decision would be made. Because of this uncertainty and the looming unknown date, it was of the upmost importance to build up a strong engaged community and to keep it going. This meant regular events and activities to connect with people and the land and to address needs. We soon realised how much the community wanted this. At the very first events we heard comments from people that confirmed this: 'I feel relaxed', 'My child is more playful and explorative in the Wood', and 'It's refreshing to meet and talk to neighbours' are just a few of the things we heard local people saying.

Through the regular community work we were able to show the decision makers that this wild space was valuable and important and that it was meeting local people's needs. We could also link our work to national policies and strategies and highlight how we were meeting these objectives through community engagement. We weren't just arguing for the *potential* of the space but the reality of how it was making a difference to people. Because we were actually delivering these ideas we could speak with complete authenticity about the value of the land for people locally.

As time went by we could also demonstrate that we were reliable and sustainable. This meant that by the time of the Public Hearing we had built up a strong network of schools, groups and local people which meant that we had no trouble getting people onto the land to support us. However, we never shared photos of the school sessions on social media or named the schools in any dealings with the press. We did not want them to feel they were a campaign tool. They were not. I knew that if we kept working with them outdoors they would see the value of the land for their children and families and they would trust that we had the community's best interest at heart. This was about creating an alternative and not a 'nimby' strategy to stop building. Our approach worked and we started to be included in school improvement plans and reports and we were mentioned in meetings. Slowly we began to build up a trusting relationship with schools and the local residents we were trying to engage with.

Because we built our community activities over a number of years people had many positive stories about the land and their time on it that they could share with the councillors and the reporter of the Public Hearing. We had spent the last number of years nurturing and collaborating with different groups so we had diverse support from within and outwith the community. This was reflected in the people supporting or attending the Public Hearing such a head teachers, local parents, wildlife organisations, community groups and our own playgroups etc. We were lucky to have people like Marguerite Hunter Blair, Chief Executive of Play Scotland, support our efforts to preserve the land for everyone. Marguerite helped us to make a film about play and the value of outdoor community spaces like the Children's Wood and North Kelvin Meadow. Marguerite also supported our idea that the land could be a test case for other areas and communities. If the building plans were rejected we could provide a model and hope for other areas. Marguerite also reinforced our argument about inequality and access to play spaces:

> Playing contributes to the wellbeing and resilience of
> all of us – the Children's Wood provides a community
> supported'environment that supports a broad range
> of opportunities for children's play and recreation.

> This is a unique community space which addresses
> the barriers to children playing outside in Glasgow,
> with a group which positively plans for increased and
> improved opportunities for play in the fourth most
> deprived Ward in Europe. There is a need for
> children to be given more opportunities to play
> outdoors with friends. . . Part of the solution outlined
> in the Play Strategy is to support parents and
> community groups in their efforts to create sufficient
> and satisfying provision of spaces for play and
> recreation within walking distance in and around
> their communities. The Children's Wood represents a
> wonderful example of community empowerment and
> engagement to meet children's need and right to play
> in an area of high deprivation.

During these years our growing organisation became a charity and, thanks to our treasurer Stephen Greenland, we secured funding and employees. These developments let the decision makers know that we were serious about what we were doing. That we were: committed, sustainable and secure. Despite all odds our guerrilla community group received funding. This also helped us to support and build community.

It wasn't all plain sailing when convincing others of this plan. Many people still said the land was dirty and unsafe. As explained earlier, previous efforts by local people had cleared rubbish and glass, but the land was still full of dog mess and many people locally hadn't set foot on the land for years, or ever for that matter. Some were still fearful of the space. One local resident said they would never come to the land – a few years into our work that person came along and loved it. There was also, despite all of the campaign's efforts, still an underlying pessimism that we wouldn't make it. I remember talking to a local community activist who said, 'It's a nice idea, but you just won't succeed – the Council need the money'. Another local person, this time a head teacher said that we 'would never succeed' and later changed this to 'well you *might* save the Wood'. This was the story. We kept meeting people from the local area and beyond who didn't believe we could win but most eventually came round to believing that we could. There were also one or two unsupportive community members who didn't understand or like the model we were adopting and so tried to undermine the campaign. The way we dealt with this was to communicate as much as possible. If there were personality clashes then we had enough people involved to mediate. A very important lesson for anyone taking on a venture like this is to recognise that you will not manage to please everyone and there will always be a minority who will object or need more communication.

Dealing with group dynamics

It is well-known that community activities are often beset with conflict. Indeed some fold under the weight of in-group conflict. Some conflict is not only normal but inevitable. In 1965 Professor Bruce Tuckman was the first to outline the four stages of group development – *forming, storming, norming, performing*. In the early days I was often aware of the storming stage which could have an impact on me and sometimes on others. When I was involved, or feeling the effect of storming, either I would step back slightly or sometimes become more involved. It all depended on what was best for the community at that time. One major thing this venture taught me is that you need to develop a thick skin when working in the community, and let things slide off. You can't take things personally when things go wrong or when disagreements occur, which inevitably they will. Any venture like this is not a bed of roses – there are a few thorny stems to negotiate and knowing this is crucial. What helps when there is conflict is to be able to get support from other people and also to be optimistic that the conflict will be short lived. As we are about to see optimism was a major feature of our campaign.

The importance of optimism

Having a strong alternative allowed us to tackle the fatalism about our chances of saving the land. But, more importantly, we needed the campaign to be optimistic. As long as people in the community, and in the campaign itself, felt pessimistic about our chances of winning then this would substantially decrease the likelihood that we would. Why bother volunteering, initiating activities or creating something if it is just going to be bulldozed by developers?

But fortunately I was very familiar with the whole issue of optimism and pessimism. Having spent years at the Centre for Confidence and Well-being and studying for an MSc in Positive Psychology I was well aware of the importance of optimism for success. Even more importantly I knew that an individual's level of optimism or pessimism is not fixed and that we can learn to become more optimistic.

The academic who has done most work in this area is Professor Martin Seligman, one of the founding fathers of Positive Psychology. In his book *Learned Optimism* he explains key differences in the thinking style of optimists and pessimists. Seligman refers to these differences as 'explanatory style'. A person's explanatory style affects how they explain good and bad events to themselves. As the box below shows there are three dimensions to explanatory style.

Box 1:
The three dimensions of explanatory style

	Pessimistic	Optimistic
Personal/ not personal	This bad thing (e.g. failing my driving test) means I'm a hopeless driver.	This bad thing (failing driving test) happened because I didn't get enough practice.
Permanent/ temporary	This bad thing will last forever (e.g. I will never pass my driving test).	This bad thing is temporary (e.g. if I get lots of practice I can pass next time).
Pervasive/ Specific	This bad thing proves that I am a useless person – a loser – and it will stop me from getting lots of jobs.	This bad thing relates to only one small aspect of my life. I'm good at doing other things and have a good life.

As we can see from this information on explanatory style when someone is pessimistic it is very easy for them to give up. This is why pessimism can become a self-fulfilling prophesy. Why should we even try if we think that failure or a bad outcome is inevitable?

An optimistic explanatory style is not simply wishful thinking or 'pie in the sky'. It is about using the facts but taking a more generous, and often realistic, perspective – one that allows for a more positive outcome. Pessimists often pride themselves on their realism but often they exaggerate the likelihood or effect of negative outcomes. For example, they will often catastrophise and make the significance of negative events much worse than they actually are.

Seligman is clear that there are times when we shouldn't try to boost optimism. These are occasions when the cost of failure is high. So we don't want an optimistic health and safety officer, for example, and we shouldn't use optimism when considering getting into serious debt. But it pays to be optimistic when it comes to education or matters of personal growth. As far as our campaign was concerned there was no great downside to us being optimistic about our prospects of winning.

So during the campaign we consciously adopted an optimistic explanatory style. Numerous times I heard stories of councillors or officials pessimistically telling people that we had no chance of success. 'There's no point in doing X because the papers have been signed,' they would say, or 'There's nothing you can do, the housing plans are already in.' These statements were not just depressing they were also incredibly effective at putting people off, especially those who didn't know the facts or the ins and outs of the planning process.

But we were ready to counter such pessimism:

- The officials are misinformed because we know they can't sign something off until planning permission is agreed.

- Just because the councillor or official was negative this time doesn't mean they will always take that view. Let's try again but let's work out a new argument.

- Just because the councillor said this about a signed document doesn't mean we are doomed and going to lose the campaign. The Scottish Government has an important role here and they are listening.

■ Look at how well we are doing with our community work. Teachers are supporting us and look at how strong our arguments are.

We also informed ourselves as much as we could on planning law and policies. This meant that we were ready to challenge councillors who told us we were wasting our time as it was 'a done deal' and we were able to tell them why they were wrong. This helped us maintain a belief that we would ultimately win. And we were right to do so as we did win in the end.

As well as consciously building an optimistic campaign we also tried to increase people's 'can do' beliefs. We created numerous leaflets and flyers with information for people to build a 'can-do' approach. Quintin, my husband, made information sheets so that people would be better informed about what was going on – the ins and outs of the campaign. For example, we had leaflets on five misconceptions about the land, and three things you need to know when speaking to a councillor. I posted these around the site, put them online, and we also put them through letterboxes.

Community events

As I've made clear throughout this book both our campaign strategy and community building idea involved putting on regular public events. These started with community gatherings, den building, and other nature and community based ideas but they quickly became more eye-catching and enticing such as lighting up the land for Halloween, bringing in real reindeer at

Christmas, or using the old floodlights during winter. In terms of a campaign strategy this kept larger numbers of people engaged with us, and at the ready if we needed them. Because we held events so regularly we were able to build up a large group of supporters quite quickly. This meant that if there was a planning related incident we could easily have people using the land and able to prove its value. For example, at our reindeer event we staged a protest and over 1,000 people joined in. They might not have come along otherwise. At these types of events we also put forward our counter-cultural ideas about how to use the space for mental health and child well-being and people began to see how the land and our community work could make a difference.

Through our events we got some great publicity. What we were doing appeared in the *Times*, the *Herald* and other newspapers. We also met up with local resident Teresa Lowe who is the literature programmer for the West End Festival and through her we became one of the festival's venues. This has led to some amazing work with authors such as Cathy Forde and Nicola Davies. Cathy has delivered creative writing projects in the Wood and said that they were the most rewarding sessions she has ever led because children and young people are much more creative and inspired when outdoors in nature. In 2018, along with local young people, she created and delivered a short outdoor performance with the youth theatre, Visible Fictions. Every year now we have a literature programme with one or two community events. These have included dog shows and galas involving local people and businesses. More recently the National Theatre of Scotland staged an outdoor production on autism, 'The Reason I Jump'. These events have not only raised our profile but also have helped to created our community. Ester and Maurizio Rossini, the then owners of North Star Café, made dinner for hundreds of children at Halloween. They generously donated both time and money. This type of support brought the community together.

I think with any campaign, seeing an opportunity in something (often, where others think none exists) and following up on it increases your chance of success. This could be an offer of help from someone or an opportunity to collaborate. It certainly meant that we were constantly busy, but it kept people engaged and provided a platform for people to be involved.

Act like you own it

Creating an alternative community on our Dear Wild Place had another huge advantage: it made it seem like we were the 'owners' of the site. We felt strongly that having access to the land and getting a community involved is a right that all local people should have. We made a very deliberate decision to 'act like we owned it'. This was an important part of the Children's Wood ethos. We acted with confidence and motivation to engage people in our alternative idea. This allowed us to easily make decisions and get things done. Being free from the owners of the land was empowering. We could think creatively without limits about how to meet our community's needs. There was no red tape or hoops to make us jump through to do the simplest of things. Red tape is often the barrier to doing the type of activities we were involved in putting on. We could test out new ideas and try out a do-it-yourself kind of style. By doing this local residents would come to believe in that it was our/ their land.

Celebrity endorsement

Another critical factor in our campaign success was, of course, celebrity support. I don't think this meant winning was inevitable but it did help us tremendously in terms of attracting wider support. For example, when the comedian, Frankie Boyle, tweeted about the campaign we had a surge in petition signatures. And that made sense as he was tweeting to 1.5 million people. As explained earlier, I got in touch with Julia Donaldson, the author of *The Gruffalo*, because I'd heard she lived (at that time) in Glasgow and I had also read articles by her about children losing touch with nature and not being able to identify natural objects. So, I found her publicist details and got in touch to see if she would support us by giving us a quote. I was fully expecting a resounding 'no' as the Children's Wood was in its infancy and we didn't have much history, but she said 'yes'. I immediately knew that this could really help us as Julia was the Children's Laureate at the time. Shortly after that Tam Dean Burn read *The Gruffalo* in the Wood and this enhanced our campaign strength. Around 200 people showed up and since then we have had a close relationship with Julia and Tam.

Involving others

Throughout this book I have explained how we tried to engage local people, schools, groups etc in what we were doing and get them involved with the land. Underlying some of this work was the idea of creating a 'tipping point'. Canadian author Malcolm Gladwell has written an inspiring book called *The Tipping Point: How little things can make a big difference*. Gladwell outlines the little things that can ultimately cause a large cultural shift in how people come to view or think about something. His theory explains why something can suddenly become a craze or a 'thing'. He shows how there is a point when the idea tips over from being the preserve of some individuals or a few groups into the wider public consciousness. He argues that ideas, products, messages and behaviours spread just like viruses do. Most people who know or work with children will know about the recent crazes for 'flossing' or 'fidget spinners'.

According to Gladwell we can work out why certain ideas go viral. The first reason is what he calls *'the law of the few'*. For an epidemic to occur there only needs to be a few very sociable people who have unusual social gifts which they use to transmit ideas and messages. But for an epidemic to happen these few need to transmit their messages to three types of people who have an important role to play in creating cultural change. He describes these types of people as follows:

■ *Connectors* – people who bring folk together and start the word of mouth chain reaction. They are usually sensitive and empathetic people who can respond to people's needs and use their sociability to break down barriers. Gladwell says that when an idea comes into contact with a Connector it has a high chance of spreading.

■ *Mavens* – people who are knowledgeable and translate that knowledge into clear messages. They remain neutral but what they say is important and people listen. In our campaign these were the people who helped to communicate important facts about the planning process or other issues on play, well-being etc.

■ *Salesmen* – people who can sell the idea by creating messages that understand how subtle things can make a difference. In their communication they pay attention to people's body language and can tailor their message to have most impact on individuals.

The second explanation for ideas going viral is what Gladwell calls *'the stickiness factor'*. A fashion or cultural shift must have something memorable at its core which means that people pay attention. In short, for a tipping point you need an idea that 'sticks'. In our campaign initially we presented the idea to everyone that this piece of land was precious as it was 'the last wild place' in our area. But there's no doubt that giving the space the name the Children's Wood had emotional resonance and made it memorable and 'sticky'.

Finally, Gladwell writes about what he calls 'the power of context'. Gladwell argues that if you want to create a tipping point where an idea really takes off then you need to create a community. Community is so important because once people are part of a group they are susceptible to information passed on through other members. As I have shown throughout this book this is exactly what we did. Because we involved lots of people we ended up with very loyal supporters and volunteers who spread the word and involved others. There were some 'early adopters' – people like Riikka Gonzales, the Grimmer family and many more who are too numerous to mention. This word of mouth grassroots initiative was much more meaningful and believable for people than simply reading a newspaper article about a campaign to save a bit of land, although there is no doubt the press coverage also helped.

My hope for this book is that it will inspire others to find their own Dear Wild Place and use it to build community and address some of the problems of contemporary society. I also hope that in these pages you have learned ways to encourage people to rally behind any campaign you may set up. But you must then value the contribution, no matter how small, of each one of these people who supports what you are trying to do with your Dear Wild Place. It is also crucially important to challenge the inevitable fatalism which often dogs campaigns, especially when you're up against a local council or multi-million pound developer. But remember, we did it and so can you – David really can defeat Goliath. ☐

References

For more references and supporting material go to the *Dear Wild Place* section of www.postcardsfromscotland.co.uk

Chapter One – Introduction

HIND, A., 1966. *The Dear Green Place*. London: Arrow Books

CRAIG, C., 2011. *The Scots' Crisis of Confidence*. Glendaruel: Argyll Publishing

CRAIG, C., 2010. *The Tears that made the Clyde*. Glendaruel: Argyll Publishing

CRAIG, C., 2012. *The Great Takeover: how materialism, the media and markets now dominate our lives.* Glendaruel: Argyll Publishing

CRAIG, C., 2017 *Hiding in Plain Sight: Exploring Scotland's ill Health* (Postcards from Scotland series) Glasgow: CCWB Press

Chapter Two – Wild space

HUGHES, A., et al. 2018. Results from Scotland's 2018 Report Card on Physical Activity for Children and Youth. *Journal of Physical Activity and Health*

KANNER, A., et al. 1995. *Ecopsychology: Restoring the Earth, Healing the Mind.* Berkeley, CA: Counterpoint Press

WILSON, E., 1984. *Biophilia*. Cambridge: Harvard University Press

KAPLAN, S., et al 2017. Directed Attention as a Common Resource for Executive Functioning and Self-Regulation. *Perspectives on Psychological Science*

ULRICH, R., et al 1991. Stress recovery during exposure to natural and urban environments. *Journal of Environmental Psychology*

New Economics Foundation https://issuu.com/neweconomicsfoundation/docs/five_ways_to_well-being?viewMode=presentation

Chapter 3 – Childhood

MOSS, S., 2012. *Natural Childhood Report*. England: National Trust

LOUV, R., 2005. *Last Child in the Woods: Saving our Children from Nature-Deficit Disorder.* Chapel Hill, NC: Algonquin Books

MACFARLANE, R., MORRIS J., 2017. *The Lost Words*. London: Penguin

TALEB, N., 2012. *Antifragile: Things that Gain from Disorder*. New York: Random House

HAIDT, J., & LUKIANOFF G., 2018. *The Coddling of the American Mind: How Good Intentions and Bad Ideas Are Setting Up a Generation for Failure*. New York: Penguin Press

KASSER, T., 2003. *The High Price of Materialism*. Cambridge: MIT press

CRAIG, C., 2012. *The Great Takeover: how materialism, the media and markets now dominate our lives* Glendaruel: Argyll Publishing

Chapter 4 – Learning outdoors

PISA., 2016. 2015 Results *(Volume I): Excellence and Equity in Education*. Paris: OECD Publishing

NICHOLSON S., 1971. How NOT to Cheat Children – The Theory of Loose Parts. *Landscape Architecture*

GARDNER, H., 1983. *Frames of Mind: The Theory of Multiple Intelligences*. New York: Basic Books

Chapter 5 – Community matters

LENGEN, C., & Kistemann T., 2012. Sense of place and place identity: review of neuroscientific evidence. *Health & Place*

PUTMAN, R., 2000. *Bowling Alone: The Collapse and Revival of American Community*. New York; London: Simon & Schuster

KASSER, T., 2003. *The High Price of Materialism*. Cambridge: MIT press

FRANKL, V., 1946. *Man's Search for Meaning*. Boston, MA: Beacon Press

LANGER, E., 2009. *Counter Clockwise Mindful Health and the Power of Possibility.* New York: Ballantine Books

LANGER, E., 2014. *Mindfulness: 25th Anniversary Edition*. Philadelphia, PA: De Capo Lifelong Books

ZEEDYK, S., 2014. *Sabre Tooth Tigers & Teddy Bears: The Connected Baby Guide to Understanding Attachment*. Dundee: Connected Baby

WILKINSON, R., & PICKETT, K., 2010 *The Spirit Level: Why equality is better for everyone.* London: Penguin Books Ltd

DORLING, D., 2011. *Injustice*. Bristol: Policy Press.

NATIONAL CHILDRENS BUREAU., 2013. *Greater Expectations: Raising Aspirations for Our Children*. London: National Children's Bureau

WORLD HEALTH ORGANISATION. *Growing Up Unequal*

EPSTEIN, R., 2007 *The Case Against Adolescence: Rediscovering the Adult in Every Teen*. Fresno, CA: Quill Drivers Books

Chapter 6 – Running a successful campaign

TUCKMAN, B., 1965. Developmental sequence in small groups. *P sychological Bulletin*

SELIGMAN, M., 2006. *Learned Optimism: How to Change Your Mind and Your Life.* New York: Vintage Books

GLADWELL, M., 2012. *The Tipping Point: How Little Things Can Make a Big Difference*. Abacus New Ed

Acknowledgements

I'd like to thank Carol Craig for her patience in waiting for me to write this book and her encouragement for me to do it in the first place. Carol has been my role model and inspiration since I began working at the Centre for Confidence & Well-being. I think she has made a real difference to Scottish culture and the ideas of the Centre underpin our community work. I am humbled to have been asked to write this book and share our story.

I have struggled in writing this book to balance our amazing journey with the underpinning theory, all the while avoiding running to many hundreds of pages! There are so many who have helped a lot or a little but for whose stories I didn't have space. I thought of writing a page of names – but there would have been hundreds and I would inevitably forget someone. To all of you, you know who you are, you know what you did, you know that your actions, little or large, have protected and shaped our wonderful Dear Wild Place and our committed, connected community. I am grateful every day for every one of us and our contribution and how each has acted on the whole and ultimately improved all of our lives. I'd like to thank our community of children, dog walkers, young people, older people, youth workers, outdoor workers, beekeepers, labyrinth walkers, treehouse builders, volunteers, gardeners, and all those who loyally love and look after the land. If it wasn't for them this story wouldn't exist.

I'd like to thank Carol Craig and Fred Shedden for editing and Derek Rodger for production. I'd also like to thank Rhiannon Van Muysen for the beautiful front cover design. Lastly, I'd like to thank my husband for putting up with my mad plans and schemes and for supporting me in the development of the Children's Wood and with the writing of the book. We spent many hours discussing the ideas in the book and his input was invaluable. I'd like to thank my children Laughlan and Jessica for embracing the outdoors when they had no other option and for providing me with a lens to see some of the issues facing children today. I'd like to thank my family for always being supportive and my mum who created nearly all of our flyers and designs for the campaign material and Children's Wood documents and helped with childcare. I'd like to acknowledge my nieces and nephews Findlay, Amy, Oisin, Isla and Euan. I hope they will have the opportunities our community has experienced in their own communities.

Finally I'd like to acknowledge those of you who are thinking of doing something like this. Go on. Do it. You will not regret it.   □

1. AfterNow – What next for a healthy Scotland?
| *Phil Hanlon/Sandra Carlisle*
The authors of this visionary book look at health in Scotland and beyond health to the main social, economic, environmental and cultural challenges of our times. They examine the type of transformational change required to create a more resilient and healthy Scotland.

2. The Great Takeover – How materialism, the media and markets now dominate our lives | *Carol Craig*
Describes the dominance of materalist values, the media and business in all our lives and how this is leading to a loss of individual and collective well-being. It looks at many of the big issues of our times – debt, inequality, political apathy, loss of self-esteem, pornography and the rise of celebrity culture. The conclusion is simple and ultimately hopeful – we can change our values and our lives.

3. The New Road – Charting Scotland's inspirational communities | *Alf Young / Ewan Young*
A father and son go on a week long journey round Scotland to see at first hand some of the great environmental, social, employment and regeneration projects which are happening. From Dunbar in the south east of Scotland to Knoydart in the north west they meet people involved in projects which demonstrate new ways of living.

4. Scotland's Local Food Revolution | *Mike Small*

Lifts the lid on the unsavoury reality of our current food system including horsemeat in processed beef products, the unsustainable movement of food round the globe, and how supermarket shopping generates massive waste. It's an indictment of a food syste that is out of control. But there is hope – the growth and strength of Scotland's local food movement.

5. Letting Go – Breathing new life into organisations | *Tony Miller/ Gordon Hall*

It is now commonplace for employees to feel frustrated at work – ground down by systems that are dominated by rules, protocols, guidelines, targets and inspections. Tony Miller and Gordon Hall explore the origins of 'command and control' management as well as the tyranny of modern day 'performance management'. Effective leaders, they argue, should 'let go' of their ideas on controlling staff and nurture intrinsic motivation instead.

Raising Spirits – Allotments, well-being and community | *Jenny Mollison/ Judy Wilkinson/ Rona Wilkinson*

Allotments are the unsung story of our times; hidden places for food, friendship and freedom from the conformity of everyday life. A fascinating look at how allotments came about; why they can make such a substantial contribution to health, well-being, community, food production, and the environment; and what's happening in other countries.

7. Schooling Scotland – Education, equity and community | *Daniel Murphy*

The Scottish schooling system does well for many children growing up in Scotland, but to ensure that all children get the education they deserve, a better partnership of parent, child, school, government and society is needed – one to which all Scotland can contribute and from which all children can benefit. Daniel Murphy suggests eight ways to ensure that Scottish education could be stronger and fairer.

8. Shaping our Global Future – A guide for young people | *Derek Brown*

Young people worry about the future world they will live in: personal futures, families and jobs. But they also worry about their global futures. The possibilities and challenges ahead appear overwhelming. This guide to human achievements and future challenges is designed to help young people consider the future their children and grandchildren will inhabit.

9. Conviction – Violence, culture and a shared public service agenda | *John Carnochan* Policeman John Carnochan takes us on a memorable journey of discovery as he comes to grips with violence and Scotland's traditionally high murder rate. He also gives a fascinating insight into the work of Scotland's Violence Reduction Unit and why it has been so spectacularly successful. This compelling book is not about high visibility policing or more officers but the importance of empathy and children's early years.

10. She, He, They – Families, gender and coping with transition | *Shirley Young*
How challenging can gender transition be for both parents and siblings? A story of hope and resilience, it shows that if parents can move beyond the shock and pain of their offspring's transition, all family members can come closer together and experience life-enhancing change.

11. Knowing and Growing – Insights for developing ourselves and others | *Alan McLean*
This extraordinary book provides insights and practical tools to help you navigate everyday human interactions, balance your own and others' needs and utilise your emotions to create a more fulfilling life. The powerful insights readers glean from 'McLean's Ring' are not only helpful for parents, teachers and leaders they are also essential for anyone aiming to encourage others to grow and develop as individuals.

12. Working for Equality – Policy, politics people |
Richard Freeman, Fiona McHardy, Danny Murphy (Editors)
Brings together 22 experienced practitioners from across the country to reflect on equality/inequality – in class, race, gender, poverty, disability and homelessness as well as health and education. They are concerned about individuals as well as ideas and policy instruments. Short and accessible, a pause for thought and inspiration for those concerned with action.

13. Hiding in Plain Sight – Exploring Scotland's ill health | *Carol Craig* Scotland. A country that prides itself on its modernity and progressive instincts. Yet this is a nation whose mental and physical health outcomes are poor by European standards. This book asks why? Grippingly readable yet challenging, Carol Craig offers an answer which is glaringly obvious. Generations of Scottish children have suffered in ways that undermine the nation's health. Starting from her own and her neighbours' lives, she explores the growing awareness internationally of the impact of Adverse Childhood Experiences.

14. Right from the Start – Investing in parents and babies | *Alan Sinclair* Scotland languishes in the second division of global child well-being. One child in every four is judged to be 'vulnerable' when they enter primary school. Alan Sinclair reveals the harm inflicted on so many of our youngest, most defenceless citizens through a toxic mix of poor parenting, bad health and a society focussed on dealing with consequences rather than causes. He also sets out a routemap for us to start putting children first by helping us all to become better parents.

15. The Golden Mean – fostering young people's resilience, confidence and well-being | *Morag Kerr (editor)* How do we encourage children and young people and help foster the skills they need to thrive in our increasingly complex world? This insightful and stimulating collection of writings by activists, people who work with the young, commentators and young people themselves provides a compelling answer. We need to strike a healthy balance between support and challenge – 'the golden mean'.

More titles are planned for 2019.
Books can be ordered from www.postcardsfromscotland.co.uk or from www.amazon.co.uk Kindle editions are also available for some titles.